SCULPTURE

for beginners

MARIA and LOUIS DiVALENTIN

BARNES & NOBLE, INC.
NEW YORK
PUBLISHERS • BOOKSELLERS • SINCE 1873

Contents

1. Getting Acquainted with Clay

Have you ever watched children making mud pies on the ground or sand castles on the beach? You yourself must have done both. Perhaps you still remember how pleased and satisfied you were with your "creation." Why not try to recapture that feeling of doing and accomplishing? It is really very simple to do and lots of fun.

BASIC SHAPES

Go to an art supply store and buy a two-pound block or brick of oil-based clay, variously called plastilene or plasticene. Now, on a table—any table, kitchen table, bridge table—unwrap your plastilene (preferably on an old newspaper, so that the table surface will not become sticky). With your thumb and index finger take a large pinch of clay, feel it between your fingers, roll it, make a round ball of it, flatten it, make a sausage shape out of it. (You will use such sausages of clay in building up heads and figures later in this book.) Now take another large pinch from your clay block and work it into the first,

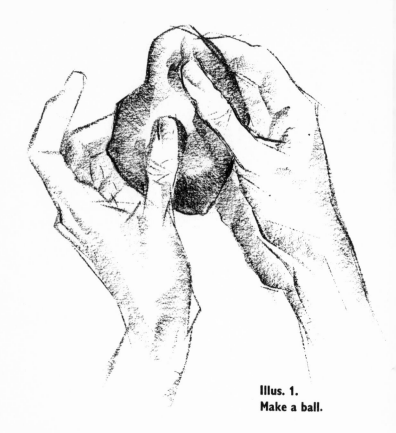

Illus. 1.
Make a ball.

making a larger ball (Illustration 1). With your thumb, press into it, make a depression, flatten it all around, press the sides, deepen the middle, make a bowl (Illustration 2). There, you've made your first piece of "sculpture."

Roll it into a ball again and keep adding from the original clay. By this time you are using all ten fingers and both hands quite busily. Try to make a perfect cube. Put it down on the table, using your thumbs (the statement, "I'm all thumbs," takes on an entirely new and significant meaning because thumbs are very important), run them along the clay, feel with them; where clay is missing add some, make little pellets and

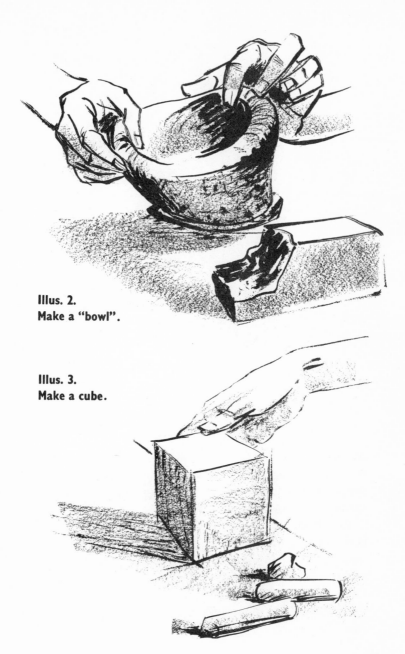

Illus. 2.
Make a "bowl".

Illus. 3.
Make a cube.

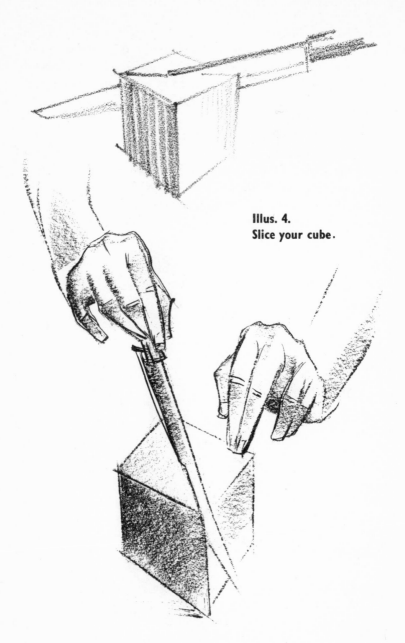

Illus. 4.
Slice your cube.

8

add them on. Where there is too much take it away. Again with the thumb make a perfectly straight edge at the top of your cube; make straight, perfect edges on all sides. All around and at each corner from top to bottom, you will have perfect 90-degree angles (Illustration 3). It is as simple as it sounds, isn't it?

With a kitchen knife cut your cube diagonally across and down (Illustration 4). You now have two wedge-shaped pieces; soften the angles, round them off a bit and bring the long sides to a point, and you have two cones. Take one cone and build it up at the pointed end, adding clay where it tapers. Add more clay where it tapers more. Now you have a cylinder.

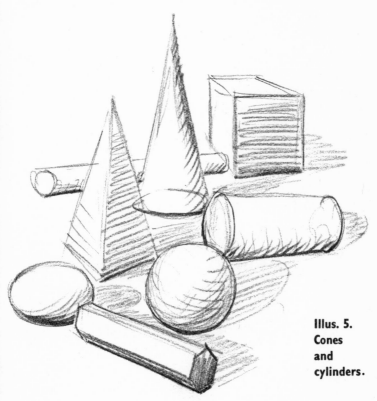

Illus. 5.
Cones
and
cylinders.

Within this short period of time you have made and experienced the basic forms used to make all the sculpture that has ever been made or that ever will be made in the future. The sphere, the cone, the cube, the cylinder, these shapes and their variations and modifications are the elementary, fundamental forms upon which all sculpture is based and created (Illustration 5).

The sculpture in this book is developed through clay models. If you are ambitious to become a full-fledged sculptor, a second Michelangelo, these are the steps that will lead you to it:

1. Clay modelling.
2. Casting in plaster.
3. Gaining a knowledge of anatomy.
4. Learning to use carving tools.
5. Developing a personal style of sculpture.
6. Working or carving creatively and directly in stone.

In this book, you will acquire a knowledge of the first three of these steps.

2. Make Some Simple Sculptures

Place an apple on a table near a window so that the light will show its form clearly and distinctly. Make sure the light falls on the side of the object you are copying at the time (Illustration 6). Let the shadows fall in back of your object or on the side. Turn your object (called the model) around as

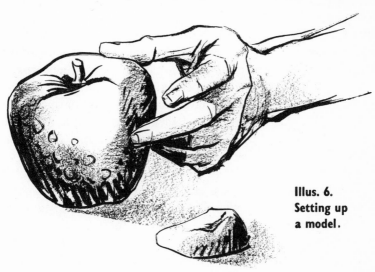

**Illus. 6.
Setting up
a model.**

Illus. 7. The apple fits into the round ball or sphere form.

you work. Also on the table, but closer to you, place a half-block of oil-based clay.

You will notice at once that the basic shape of the apple is spherical (Illustration 7). So start by working your clay into as round a shape as possible. Take pieces of clay and make them into sausage or bat-like forms; then put them together, bend them, join them. Use your hands and your fingers; press the clay firmly together until you have it as nearly ball-shaped as possible. Now, look at your model again. How does it really look at the top? Does the central part recede, does it go down in the middle? How far? With your thumb dig out some of the clay. Dig the deepest point in the middle and less deeply around it. When you get to the upper part surrounding the middle, here dig still less, until you have reached the crest or uppermost part, which then curves up and then comes down and around to form the outer mass. Look at the apple again. Notice the kind of curve from the innermost deepest point (middle top) up to the uppermost point and down the sides. Using your fingers, duplicate this curve in the clay. But notice that the shape of the curve will change the moment you look at the apple from another viewpoint. You will also note that the crest of the curve will vary or even undulate slightly. Look at the apple all around—you still see that it is quite uneven. One side of it may be flatter than the other. One side may be larger and rounder than the other. Also, the circumference at the top of the apple will be different from the circumference in the middle and that at the bottom. The lowest part will be fluted and bumpy. Notice how many bumps. How far do they go in and out? The underpart of the apple is also fluted and has a recessed middle not as deep, however, as the one at the top.

Where the shape of the apple is fuller the clay will need filling out, so make clay pellets by rolling a bit of clay with your thumb and index finger and add them by pressing them firmly into the clay. Where the shape of the apple is less full, remove some of the clay. Add where you need to build up the mass; subtract where the form is too full. Press the pellets in firmly with your thumb. You can add one pellet over the other or next to the other until you have the required shape. Don't slick over or smooth out—this is a tendency of all novices. Press in harder with your thumbs where you want to indent; your thumbs will gain strength and ingenuity. If you keep comparing your clay apple with nature's product you will have eventually moulded the clay to look like the real thing. Put a stem into the top middle of your clay apple. Roll a small piece of clay into a tiny cylinder and attach it in there—bend it slightly for realism.

Illus. 8. When you model any fruits or vegetables, determine beforehand into which basic geometric form it fits. You will then be able to use your clay more successfully and far more easily than if you flounder around and try to find the shape eventually. Characterize each one —is it a cube, a cone, a cylinder, a sphere?

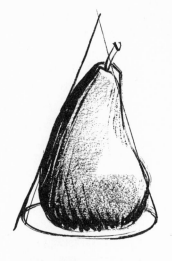

Illus. 9.
The pear is
basically cone-shaped.

THE PEAR

Now go on to the next form (Illustration 9). The pear resembles most closely the cone; where it varies from it, remove some clay and curve it if necessary. It may need to curve out on one side and in on the other. At the base it will curve in and under. Mould it, shape it, press it into the shape you want.

THE CARROT

Do the same thing with the carrot (Illustration 10). First, determine its basic geometric form, which in this case is the cylinder. Now, roll your clay first into a tube-like shape. This is very simple. You can roll it on the table with your hand; roll it back and forth until it looks like a cylinder. Taper one

Illus. 10. The carrot
fits into a cylindrical form.

end by removing some clay. Build up the thickness of the opposite end, round it over and at the top allow for the stalks sprouting out of the root.

THE PEPPER

With the pepper, too, determine beforehand that its shape is fundamentally that of a cube, modified with variations (Illustration 11). Notice the sections and indentations, the curves along the top, the sides and the bottom. Add clay to fill out the form and remove it where the shape is indented and recessed. Note the *in* areas and the *out* areas and the *in between* areas. Always remember to roll pellets with your thumb and index finger. Flatten them, and then apply them firmly to your clay model where you want to add to and fill out the form.

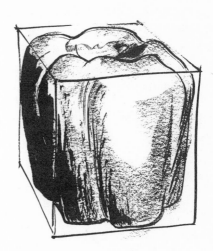

**Illus. 11.
The pepper
is fitted
easily into a
cube form.**

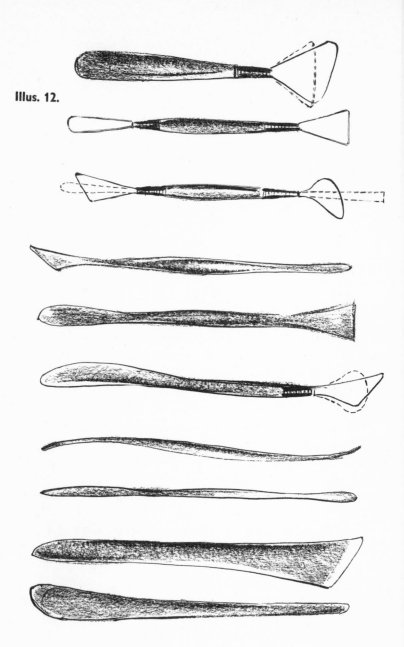

Illus. 12.

3. Tools You Will Be Using

After you have worked with the basic shapes and have experimented with modelling simple objects, and you feel you know the clay—that is, that you can make it do what you want it to do—perhaps you may want to buy some real clay modelling tools. Tools will help you to attain what you want more easily and directly.

The tools that are shown in Illustration 12 are those generally used for clay modelling of less than life-size pieces. Use looped wire tools to cut away, subtract, remove, and to make hollows and concave areas. The all-wood stick tools can be used to add clay to the model, for flattening it into place, and for "drawing" in the clay.

The sizes of the wire loops vary according to the size and kind of excavated hollow that is required. The small wooden sticks are used to add clay in small, detailed places and parts. The larger wire tools are used to establish wide planes and areas, while the larger wooden ones are used to add larger quantities of clay to your model. The smaller wire tools are used to dig out in smaller areas and places like the corner of the eye, the

17

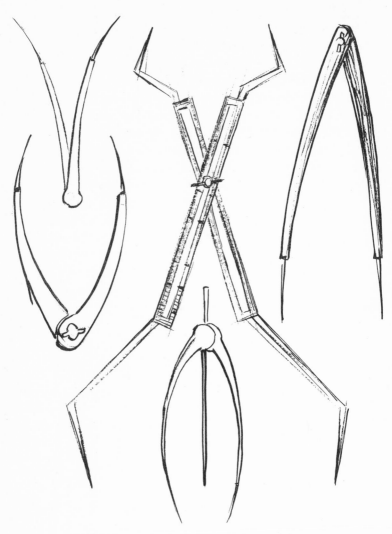

Illus. 13. Calipers and proportional dividers.

opening in the ear, etc. Calipers are used for measuring, and proportional dividers are necessary whenever you want to reduce or enlarge an object you are copying (Illustration 13).

Remember that tools are useful, but a wide assortment of tools will not automatically make you a good sculptor. There is no substitute either for the tool described by professional sculptors as "an educated thumb."

Besides these few simple things, if you like, you can invest in two used stands—one to hold your model and one to work on. These stands have a rotating top and are adjustable in height. They also have casters and can be easily pushed around so you can view your work from different angles and in different lights. Most sculptors make or improvise their own tools and equipment according to their needs and the requirements of a specific piece of sculpture. For example, you can make an excellent stand from a high stool with a revolving seat. If the stool is not high enough for you, extend the length of the legs by nailing lengths of wood to them. A revolving table-top trivet can be pressed into service as a modelling stand for smaller pieces and used on a table of appropriate height.

Illus. 14. Revolving stands.

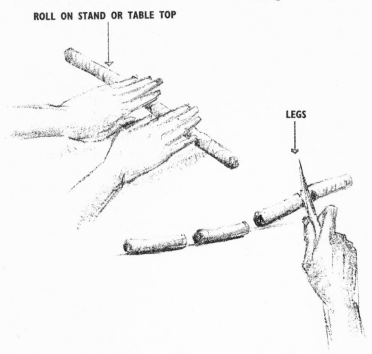

ROLL ON STAND OR TABLE TOP

LEGS

4. Make Some Figures

You are now ready to make figures using the basic shapes you have learned about.

BEAR

Try doing some small pieces of sculpture which do not require an armature or skeleton inside them. If the figure is done compactly it will easily hold itself together without need of internal support. Start with your clay, working it into small sausage-like shapes. Work these together to form a ball for the head of a bear, a larger egg-shaped form for the body, and two triangular clay parts for the ears (Illustration 16). Most of these

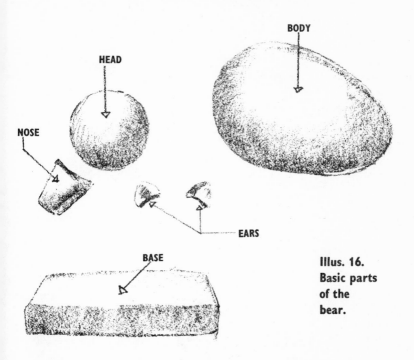

Illus. 16. Basic parts of the bear.

preparatory stages and parts require only the deft use of your hands and fingers. When you put the "head" and body together, use a wooden tool all around the joining-edges, working one form into the other. Your wooden tool will seal the sphere-like head to the egg-shaped body. If there is too much clay where the two have been connected, you can cut it away with a wire tool. Tools never eliminate the use of the fingers: Wherever

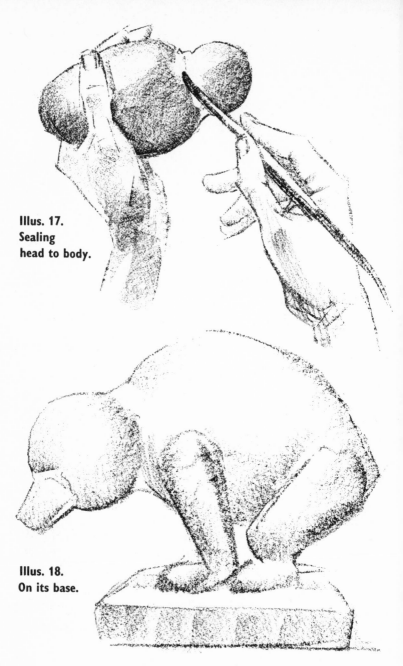

**Illus. 17.
Sealing
head to body.**

**Illus. 18.
On its base.**

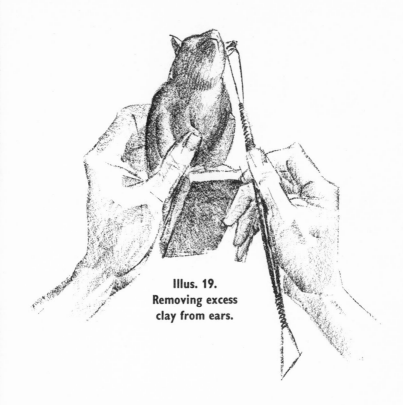

Illus. 19.
Removing excess
clay from ears.

you think they can be used to imprint, indent or build up your form, use your fingers.

When you attach the ears, hold the head in position with one hand and work the clay in with the other. Then you can use your wire tool to straighten out the clay if there is more of it than you need. If there is not enough, roll clay pellets and apply them firmly with your fingers. You can press them further with a wooden tool and smooth the edges so they become part of the main area you are working on.

The outer parts of the ears can be cut and formed by a wire tool, while the indentations in the inner portion can be pressed in and modelled with a wooden tool, to convey a quality of smooth softness.

Illus. 20. The finished bear.

DACHSHUND

A small dachshund would make a charming and simple sculpture piece. You need not try for too much realism, but hold in mind basic geometric forms—an oblong block for the body, a rounded modified sphere for the head with a cone for the nose. After you have pressed together your worked clay into a rectangular block, use your large, straight wire tool to modify the form and cut away the excess clay. Afterwards, use your wooden tool to soften the edges, to round off, to blend, to mould. Scoop out the place for the eye with a small rounded

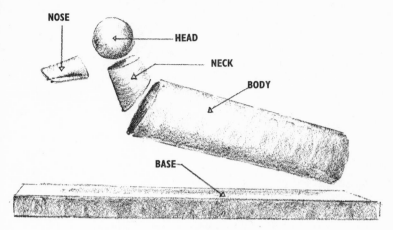

Illus. 21. The parts of the dachshund.

wire tool. Now make a ball of clay by rolling some between your fingers, then place it into the scooped-out area. With your small wooden tool gently spread the edges of the ball all around

Illus. 22. The smaller parts of the dachshund.

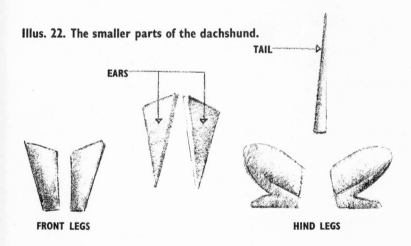

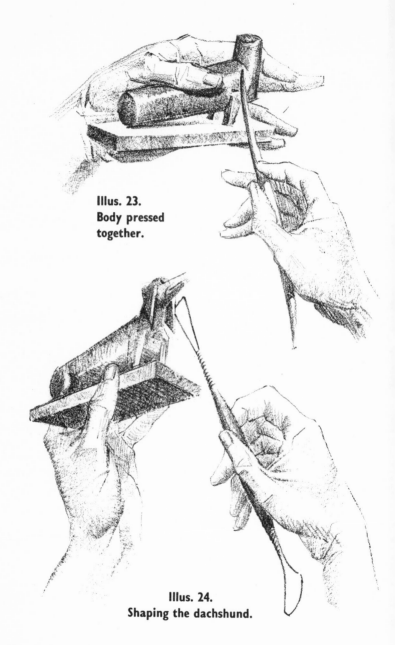

Illus. 23.
Body pressed
together.

Illus. 24.
Shaping the dachshund.

Illus. 25.
The finished dog.

so that it takes its place in the head as part of the unit. Make a small cylinder-like tail and attach it to the end of the body; shape long floppy ears and join them at the sides of the head; modify the form of the nose, etc.

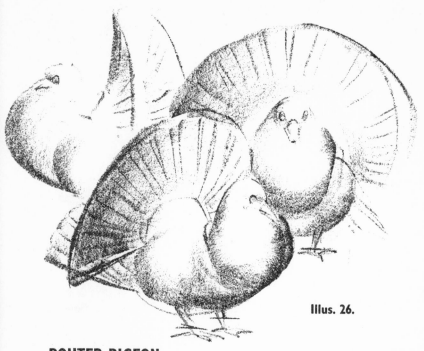

Illus. 26.

POUTER PIGEON

Try a pouter pigeon. Make a small round ball of clay, then a larger one, then join them, model a fan-like tail. Block it out separately and flatten it with your fingers, and taper it at the outer edge. Cut the curves with your wire tools. You can easily do a decorative feather design on it by making consecutive radial indentations with your wire tool. Press the tool firmly into the clay, and instead of lifting it directly, drag the tool along a bit, using a less-firm pressure. Keep repeating this until you have a series of step-like indentations and designs in your clay. The sphere which denotes the head can be scooped out into a bowl-shaped, negative form. You use a large round wire tool to do this; then smooth the recessed surface with your fingers and a wooden tool. Experiment with your tools, try them out, see what each one can do.

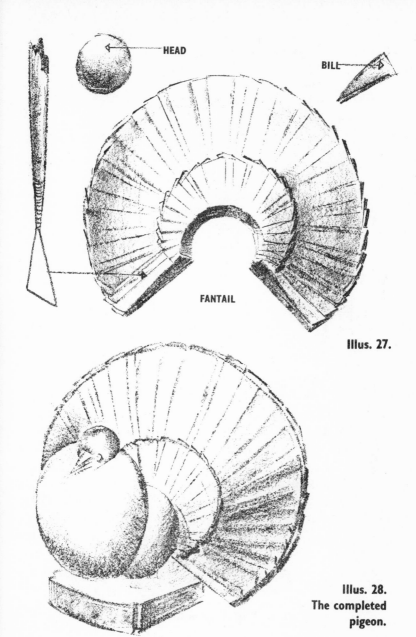

HEAD

BILL

FANTAIL

Illus. 27.

Illus. 28.
The completed
pigeon.

29

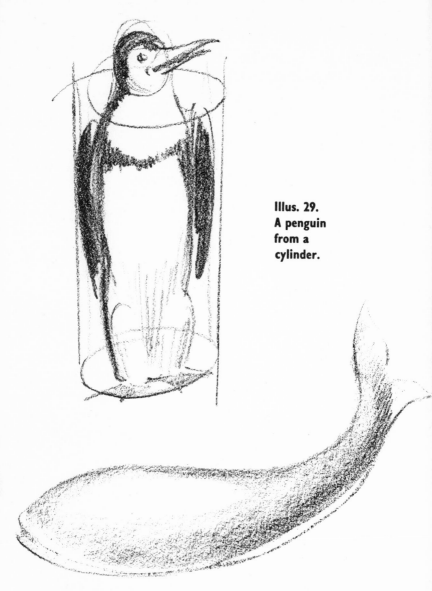

Illus. 29.
A penguin
from a
cylinder.

Illus. 30. A whale from two cylinders.

FEMALE FIGURE

Make a small female statue, with not too much detail and with the accent on general outline and simple design. You will principally use an elliptical, elongated form, with a smaller egg shape for the head, attached by a short cylinder-form neck to the extenuated body. Use your wooden tools to join one part to the other. Use your wire tools to scoop out areas. Make the body concave rather than a realistic convex shape. The inner surface, after having been excavated with round wire tools, can be smoothed or moulded with wooden tools. Add drapery if you are ambitious. (Consult pages 133 through 135.) Drapery is always added on, not tooled out. Make high ridge lines and low recessed curves. To distribute clay evenly along a line, use a wire tool. To blend, mould, smooth and flatten, use a wooden tool. (See next page.)

Illus. 31. With scales and fins, your whale can be a fish.

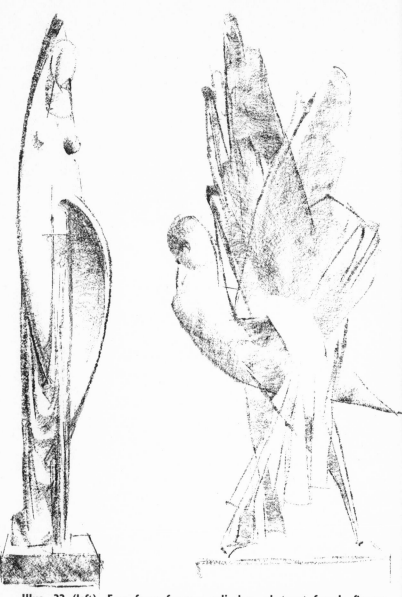

Illus. 32 (left). Free form from a cylinder—abstract female figure.
Illus. 33 (right). Free form—bird in flight.

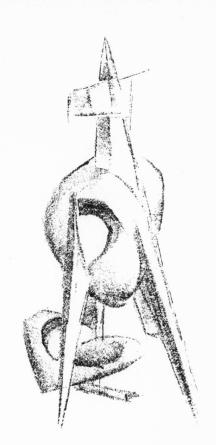

Illus. 34.
Free form
from a
pyramid.

ABSTRACT FORM

Try doing an imaginative and more complicated abstract by super-imposing and interlocking various forms that you create. They need not resemble actuality. Use shaped-hole-in-air areas to complement or take the place of filled-in areas. Mass can counter open space. An outer egg-shaped mass can contain a spherical air-space. A pyramid can be joined by flattened squares and topped by a cube. A cylindrical form can join a cone. An infinite number of expressions and interpretations are possible. Try them.

5. Decorating Your Home with the Objects You Make

You have bought some clay and you have acquired a few basic clay-modelling tools. Perhaps you even now own a pair of calipers and a stand (or two). You have already made the few basic shapes and the elementary forms. You find yourself at an impasse.

"What shall I make?" is an age-old question at this point. Or perhaps your problem can be better stated as "What can I do with what I make?" The amateur often finds himself unable to decide what to make only because he doesn't yet recognize the avenues that are open to him to use his creations as decorations.

At one time sculpture was an important part of everyday life. In ancient Greece and Rome, sculpture was one of the commonest forms of artistic expression and of home decoration. Even down through the Renaissance, sculpture was an accepted part of everyday life. It was only with the rise of the graphic arts (like painting, engraving, lithography and printing)

Illus. 35. In the background can be seen a standing bronze figure against a pale grey wall. In the middle against the bookshelves is a reclining female figure in bronze on a white rug. The left foreground contains white plaster figures near a redwood wall.

that sculpture fell into a decline. Fortunately, people everywhere are now recognizing the decorative value of sculpture in the home and a revival is under way. Once you start to create sculpture for the specific purpose of decorating your home, you will be amazed to find how many new and as yet undiscovered places can accommodate the things you make.

When you display the things you make, there will be no need for pedestals. Think of your sculpture as complementing your furnishings. Any flat surface that will hold your sculpture will do nicely. A cocktail table is excellent for a small piece and so

Illus. 36. The small sculpture on the piano is a patined bronze set on a dark wood surface. The white abstract on the red quarry tile floor has been left in its original plaster finish.

Illus. 37. (Seen from the other side.) The small piece is on the piano and the larger abstract on the floor.

Illus. 38. Here a large piece of sculpture is placed on the steps leading from one area to another. The figures are silhouetted against a translucent movable screen.

The sculptures can be seen both from the upper dining area and the lower studio level. This is ideal placement, for it makes possible so many points of view, and relates the sculptures in the foreground and background, effecting a feeling of unity and composition.

is a shelf or a bookcase. Reserve the floor for larger pieces that can blend with the interior decoration of the room. You can place a piece on a dresser or hang a bas relief on the wall. Experiment with placement. Place your sculpture in the most suitable area where it becomes part of the surroundings.

Plan the lighting, too. If your piece of sculpture is finished in stone or marble, silhouette it against something dark. If it

Illus. 39. The life-size torso (left) is placed flatly on the floor at the edge of a partition. It designates not only the end of the entrance hall but leads into a recessed dining area.

is finished in bronze, place it against a lighter background. Often you can enhance a bronze piece by placing it near or on a darker or lighter wooden chest or table. Try it near contrasting textures or complementary colors. Even window sills can be used if they are wide enough and with an interesting changing light. Use a piece of sculpture with a painting. This arrangement often enhances both pieces. You may even want to place a large piece in the center of a room. Of course, a large room is the first requirement. And the sculpture must be such as to warrant this kind of placement. It should be compact and at least life size. If it has a solid flat base of its own, it won't need a block or stand under it for support. It can be the focus and most dramatic thing in a room or it can be used as an understatement.

Always try to relate your sculpture to tables, chairs, windows, doors, and walls. Do not overcrowd. Select the location with

Illus. 40. "Meditation" fits between two portraits.

Illus. 41. Small terra-cotta figure of musician is on glass-topped buffet. Middle right is a bronze plaque on the redwood wall.

Illus. 42. An oval piece with a counter oval stand in gold leaf is placed under a glass brick window. And a miniature torso, gold patined, is set on a dark walnut chest.

the size and the shape of the sculpture in mind. A piece of sculpture can be used at the entrance to an area or it can be used to lead the eye from one area to another. Sculpture can be used as a room divider, or it can become part of the wall itself. Experiment with hanging a bronze plaque on a white wall or place a dark bronze figure against stark white plaster. Use pink marble with cherry wood. Use bronze with clear plastic or against a wall of colorful books. Group pieces of sculpture. Smaller pieces can be placed together on a table or dresser.

If you come to dislike a location, you can always find another. One thing is certain—your home will never be dull, because sculpture lends cultural excitement to your life and surroundings. It enhances and enriches with continued enjoyment and attractiveness.

Your experience with sculpture will not only add to your pleasure and understanding of beauty and its expression, but it will also open to you many new worlds. The museums, the art exhibits, architecture and travel, all these will become a part of your life and will take on new meanings for you.

6. Learning from Plaster Casts

Now that you know some of the uses to which your handiwork can be put, you can go on to the next step. Obtain some small plaster casts (of the type traditionally used in art schools), which you can purchase at any artist's materials or supply shop. Or perhaps you will be able to borrow them from your school art department.

Begin by copying parts of the anatomy. It is easiest to start with the foot. Work in a clear strong light that will give you plenty of shadow. Light and shadow give visible form to your work. Of course, the ideal place to do sculpture is in a large studio with a high ceiling that has a skylight in it. But if this is not feasible for you, a wide window facing north will do. You can have the window shades attached so that they draw up from the bottom, and your work will have the benefit of the upper half of the light.

THE FOOT

The foot can be said to resemble a rectangular block with a column or cylindrical shape set into it toward the back end of the block (Illustration 43). The foot is made up of rather flat

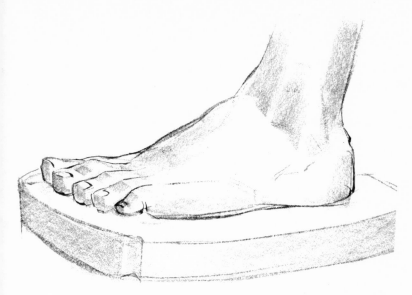

Illus. 43. Plaster cast of the foot.

areas and planes; the rear inside comes down seemingly in a line extending from the leg and ankle. The heel itself extends in back beyond the leg column. The instep joins the front of the leg almost at a right angle when the foot is flat on the ground. The major portion of the foot before you get to the toes slopes down towards the outer edge. The planes that form the foot are broad, and fairly simple to model. Look at your own foot; check its length; where does the leg column set into it?

The toes are small varied cylinders, modified and rounded off at the ends. The joints in the toes are shorter and thinner than those in the fingers except for the big toe—this one lacks a joint just as the thumb does. The tip of the big toe turns up and while it is separated from the other toes it is not set at an angle like the thumb is from the fingers.

The heel makes up the outer back part of the foot while a saddle-shaped bone forms the inner part. The under side of

this saddle-shaped bone rests on the forward part of the heel bone, the rest of the heel goes back and down. Notice the length of the foot goes back quite far behind the ankle. In between the heel, saddle and the instep bones are four smaller bones that make the bridge or arch; when you walk these bones never touch the ground. Make sure you cut and curve this arch highest at the inner edge and down to the front ball of the foot. This bridge is less and less arched as you go from the inner to the outer edge, where the foot touches the ground all along that side from little toe back to the heel.

The part of the lower leg which joins the foot is basically a round cylindrical form. Make sure the outside ankle bone is lower down into the foot than the inside ankle bone. Take a close observant look at your foot, your ankle, your toes. How do they relate to each other? How much lower is the outside of your foot as compared to your instep? How fast does your instep turn in under the arch? How does the heel round under? Look at the illustration, notice the length of the foot—notice where the ankle enters (refer to Chapter 10).

While extensive copying from plaster casts is undesirable, some copying is absolutely necessary to train the eye to see and the hand to do. You will also have the advantage of being able to come back to it whenever you choose to or have the time. You will not have to complete it within a certain period nor will its position change, as would be the case if you were working from life. Learn to walk away from your sculpture; step back; take a long look at it. Walk around, then come back to it. Rotate the upper stand. Have you been giving as much attention to the sides and all around? Learn to do this from your very first piece. It is one of the most valuable habits you can acquire. You will find that doing sculpture can be both fascinating and exhausting. You will also discover that there is never quite enough time. Sculpture becomes an absorbing interest that requires concentrated effort and attention, since it involves not only the senses of sight and touch but also judgment, interpretation and imagination.

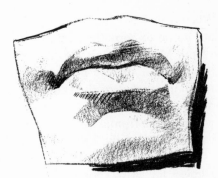

Illus. 45. Plaster cast of the mouth.

THE MOUTH

As you can see, the upper lip is made up of three masses, the central mass is peaked in the middle foreground, brought up from either side. The two side masses are formed from below the inner to above the upper bow curved outline. The lower lip consists of only two masses that come together in the middle to form a soft valley where the peaked parts of the upper lip fits into it. The mouth is formed over the arch of the teeth and so must follow this contour. Therefore, the corners of the mouth are quite deep and far back, covering the area of the molars beneath them. There is neither a line nor a straight line between the upper and the lower lip, which are actually separate forms. You will notice that both lips are indented by a ridge all around the edges where the red part of the lips ends and the white skin of the face begins. Look at your own mouth in the mirror. How does it differ from that of Michelangelo's statue of David? What similarities are there?

A few additional comments about sculpting a mouth: Never make it a flat plane. Think of the arch of teeth under it; the closest part to you will be the middle peak, and the two sides will recede and go back towards the ear lobes. Think of the corners of the mouth as part of a larger curve which continues beyond the corners of the mouth back to the base of the skull.

THE EYE

When you have these concepts clearly established in your mind, go on to copy the human eye. Again using a cast of the eye from Michelangelo's David, the first thing you will realize is the fact that the eye itself is a ball. Like a ball, it is fitted into a bony socket in the skull. It protrudes from the socket, and the upper lid covers and protects it. The lid itself extends down from the frontal bone. This bone comes forward beyond the upper part of the eyeball. Note the relationships between the frontal bone, the eyebrow, the upper lid, the eyeball, and the lower lid. Also, notice that the inner corner of the eye where the two lids come together differs considerably from the outer corner. The curve of the upper lid is quite different from the curve of the lower lid.

Always remember that although you are working with inert clay, you are trying to simulate the structure of a human eye

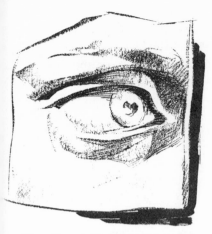

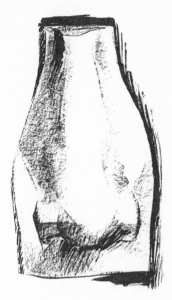

Illus. 46 and 47. Plaster cast of the
eye and nose.

placed in a skeletal bony skull, covered by lids, made of muscles
and skin, and having form and thickness.

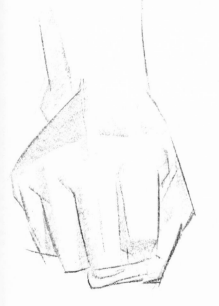

Illus. 48 and 49. Plaster cast
of the fist and ear.

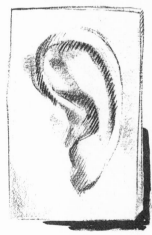

If by this time you have had enough of copying parts of the body, you may want to do a whole head. Get a cast of a Greek or Roman head to copy before you attempt a portrait head from life. The structure of the usual classical male head with strong prominent features will be less difficult for you at this time.

Begin as always with an armature. In the case of a comparatively straight head all you will need is a simple flat board with an upright perpendicular stick in the middle. Make a number of clay sausages and put them on, firmly packed, around the upright. Keep adding and thumbing them on until you have a clay mass approximating the size of the head you are copying. A point to remember—in fact, a very important point—is the axis of the head. No matter how rigidly straight, the least tilt sideways, to the front or backward will deviate it from a true perpendicular. (Every form has its own axis.) Always establish this axial or pivotal center. You can do this very easily by drawing a line up through the middle of the face up to the top of the head and down to the middle of the neck at the back. Then draw another line starting from one side up again to the top of the head and down the other side. Now where the two lines intersect at the top is the true midpoint or axial point (Illustrations 50 through 52). You can mark this with a toothpick or thin nail in the clay. Work outwards from this guide. It will help you to make the left and right halves of the head symmetrical.

You can mark the cast at different points with a pencil and then with the help of your calipers try to find or establish the same measuring points on your clay mass. Always measure. At this stage, your sense of observation will not be developed enough to detect disproportions. So, besides the larger, more general measurements, such as from top of head to base of neck, take in-between measurements, such as top of head to brow; from bridge of nose to tip; from top of head to top of

**Illus. 50.
The head
in clay.**

**Illus. 51.
Finding the
axial point
or mid-point.**

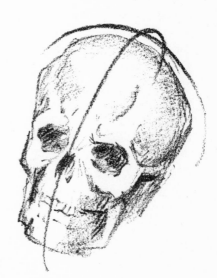

Illus. 52.

ear; and from top of the ear to lobe. Measure all around and up and down, and don't neglect the back of the head. One word about finishing: The novice is always anxious to finish, to put in the details. Never be concerned with the details until the very end. Always be concerned with the large mass and the forms. Always use a broad treatment, never a detailed one. Think in terms of basic units and geometric shapes, and you will easily maintain a feeling of control.

Leave some time from sculpture for sketching or drawing. Sit down with paper and pencil and try to put what you see in black and white. You may find that you will flounder. In the beginning it may be somewhat discouraging but keep at it. Draw anything, everything—a chair, a table, a tree, a book, clouds, a dog—anything in your line of vision. This training will be invaluable. Try to remember how objects look to you, and draw them from memory. This is the most difficult but the best way to stimulate and develop your "inner vision," the imagination. You will find that the accumulation of your experiences in sketching will help you in your sculpture. It will make you aware of the existence of forms everywhere. Your sketch book will become your storehouse of notes for future use in expressing yourself more clearly, more beautifully, more accurately, more closely to that ideal which every artist strives for but never quite realizes. For, as Browning says, "A man's reach should exceed his grasp."

7. Using the Armature for Support

Any time that you set out to make more than just a small head, you will need an armature. An armature is an understructure. It holds the clay up and on, and keeps it from slipping and dropping down. This skeletal, or under, form can consist of a thick flat piece of board, with an upright piece of pipe screwed into the middle. An elongated, elliptical wire is looped at the top of the pipe. The armature should resemble, in a very simple and crude way, the object you plan to sculpt or put over it. It is a support and must therefore be adequate to hold up the clay that you are going to place on it. If you are going to do a head with shoulders and torso, your armature must be constructed with a strong, flat baseboard and a heavy lead pipe upright in the middle. At the top of this, place your looped wire for the head. Now place a crossbar below the neck where the shoulders will be. Do this by winding a piece of copper tubing at the middle with the two ends of the tubing extending out. Two more bars cross the perpendicular to support the torso and diagonal ones from the outermost points to the middle, or, in other words, from outer hip to

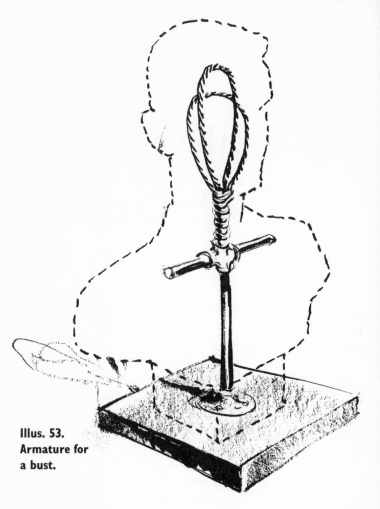

**Illus. 53.
Armature for
a bust.**

inner groin. The armature will vary, depending on the pose
and shape. Simple armatures can be purchased at art supply
shops. The professional sculptor makes his own, using all
sorts of things from chicken wire, lumber and burlap to
plaster and bricks. He knows best what he needs and how
to prepare the under frame for the composition he has in
mind.

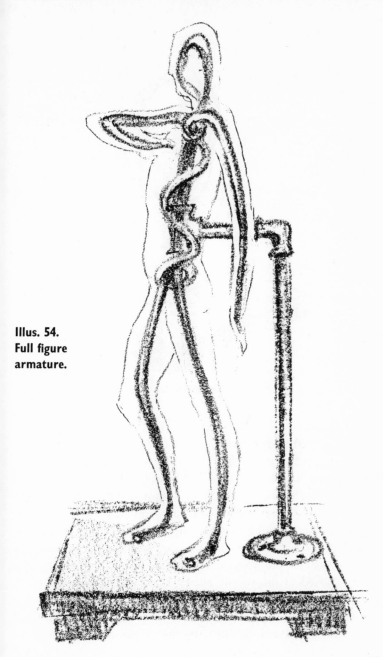

**Illus. 54.
Full figure
armature.**

Illus. 55. Armature for a head.

If you are at all ingenious, you may want to try to improvise and use whatever is handy to build an understructure yourself. Just be sure it is sturdy, that it will not fall apart, and that it will hold up the clay. Also, make sure it is not bigger than the piece of sculpture you plan to create over it, or it may extend beyond your intended design. This happens more often than you think—and to professionals, too, who must then saw and hack away at the excess. Although simple armatures can be purchased at art supply shops, making one yourself takes only a little time and trouble, and is worth it. There is nothing more frustrating than to spend hours sculpting an ambitious piece only to have it fall into an amorphous clay mass because no armature supports its weight. If your sculpting time and labor are important to you, take the small additional time necessary to give your piece the internal support it needs. You will find it well worth the trouble.

If making an armature is too much for you, however, buy a ready-made one at your art supply shop. They are available in various sizes to support heads, busts, full human figures, and animals.

(Also see page 129)

8. Making a Head in Clay

After your experience with basic forms and with copying parts of the anatomy from plaster casts, you will be ready to try something more ambitious, like a head. (If your attempt involves a less-than-life-size head, without neck and shoulders, then you can probably proceed without first building an armature or skeletal form beneath the clay.) Before you begin, it is best to acquaint yourself with the shape of a head. Pictures of a head will do for this. These you can get at any art supply shop and better still, you can also buy a skull. This is excellent for studying the bone structure under the muscle, flesh and hair that cover it. However, if you are not prepared to spend time in this kind of study then you can do your observing from life, by looking at yourself in a double mirror or getting someone to pose for you. Make sure you really look at your sitter's head from all sides and all around. Look at the shape, spend at least a few minutes studying proportions. How far from the top of the head are the eyes? What is the distance between the eyes? Measure. Use your calipers. Where does the nose begin with reference to the eyes? Where does it stop?

Illus. 56. Prepare your armature and work the clay into manageable lengths beforehand.

What is the distance between the tip of the nose and the uppermost part of the upper lip? Is the corner of the mouth in a perpendicular line with the pupil of the eye? Do the distances from the nostril to the eye to the lobe of the ear form a triangle?

Illus. 57. Mass the clay on to the armature. Use your hands to thump it on. Put on as much as needed to approximate the eventual size.

This sort of visual awareness of proportions, shapes and sizes and their relationships is of the greatest importance. You will come to this conclusion yourself if you are seriously interested in what you are doing.

Let us assume that you have chosen a sitter, preferably you, and you plan to do head, neck and upper shoulders.

Your armature must be prepared accordingly. Instead of a simple, elongated, elliptical loop on top of a pipe, prepare a sturdier armature, one that will sustain the extra clay weight of neck and shoulders. The advantage of the wire armature for a head is that even after you have the clay on, you can still tilt or change the position because of its flexibility. But here you are more concerned with strength, so choose a wooden armature (Illustration 56). Now prepare your clay sausages. Start to pack the clay onto the armature (Illustration 57). For a self-portrait, you will have to work with mirrors. Place them so you will get side and back views of yourself. Take measurements as soon as you have a large enough mass to approximate the size. Establish some critical points. First, the pit of the neck to the top of the head. In profile, establish the slant from the back of the head to the jaw line and from the back of the head to the nose. Notice, in profile, that the end of the skull in back is in line with the tip of the nose. Keep this in mind at all times, because it is one of the mistakes that occurs most often. Establish the length of the indentation from the point of the chin to the top of the throat in front. Measure the length of the neck, its width, its thickness. Note especially (in profile) the slant of the base of the neck from back to front. Establish the width of the shoulders. Thicknesses from front to back of shoulders vary at different points.

Once you have arrived at these measurements you can either jot them down or put toothpicks in the clay itself, to mark them off. Be guided by these indicators as you add or subtract the clay. Try to work all around and up and down. Turn the clay often. And don't forget the back of your portrait is as important as the front. Remember what you have learned about the structure of the skull. Go back and take another look. Never make the face or eyes flat. The face is an oval. The eyes are not on the surface. Dig the socket first. Dig deeply into the clay. Don't be timid, you can't spoil anything (Illustration 58). The eyeballs are modelled afterwards, separately

Illus. 58. With your wire tool dig out the eye sockets under the brow. Establish the central line from the sternum up through the neck, chin, mouth, nose, forehead, over the top of the head and down the back.

and laid into the sockets. The eyelids are put on over the eyeballs. Don't put too much realism in the eyeball. Don't

Illus. 59. With your wire tools find the large planes, establish the high points; measure distances. Relate the different parts to each other.

incise it, even if you are trying to show the fact that it is a very dark eye. Don't bore in to show or designate the pupil—it will result in a black shadow. Give attention to the shape and form of the eyeball and later you can lightly trace the outline of a pupil, if you must.

If you are going to move the position of the head, the whole case, the entire skull, moves in the direction chosen. It moves. It pivots on its axis as a unit on a springy column.

Tip your head back and look at yourself in the mirror. You will see that both sides of the face slope down, back and around from the central ridge. The chin, teeth and eyes all follow the horseshoe shape, and curve in the same way. Use your wire tool on the clay to establish large planes and curves (Illustration 59).

Make the bridge of the nose definite and strong. Don't place the eyes too close together. Another thing to remember about the nose is that it is set into the face as much as it sticks out from it. In profile, the middle part of the nose where it starts to jut out is in line with the tip of the upper lip. In fact the upper lip grows out from under the half-way mark between the tip of the nose and the innermost part of the nostril. The corner of the mouth generally is in line with the inset of the nose, depending on the arch of the teeth and the width of the mouth. Remember that the mouth always follows the shape of this arch (Illustration 58).

Each side of the nose slopes down from the ridge and continues circling under the eyes to form the under-half edge of the eye socket, then broadens at the outer high cheek point that goes on to form the zygomatic arch leading back to the ears (Illustration 60).

The nose narrows a bit past the bony part and sinks slightly towards the cartilaginous bulb which flares out on each side to form the nostrils. The middle of the bulb and the tip of the nose curves under, back, and leads down into the middle of the groove of the upper lip (white-skin lip portion). The end of the nose has many small planes and delicate curves that

Illus. 60. Make the high point of the zygomatic definite. Place the ear properly in relation to the jaw, to the brow and the nose.

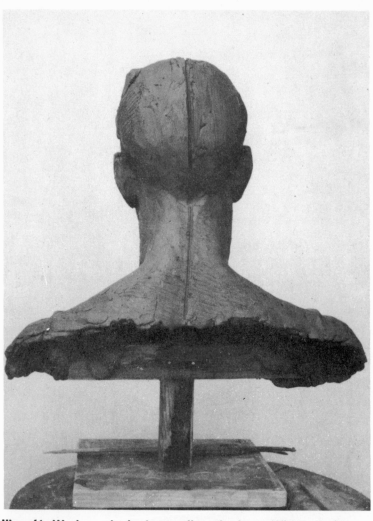

Illus. 61. Work on the back as well as the front. With your fingers make clay pellets and add them on where needed. Make sure the base of the skull overhangs the base of the neck.

Illus. 62. With your wooden tool add clay and press it in, using your fingers too. The hair is treated as a mass and grows out of the skull.

require definite modelling. The openings in the nose are not round. Many novices make this mistake.

Never think of the mouth as a line, but as a muscle. A lower and upper thick, flexible muscle. Remember that the shape of the upper and lower jaws controls the shape of the mouth. If the jaws are curved much in front, the more the lips will be curved over them. The lower and upper lips are quite different from each other. The lower lip is rounded and has a central groove separating two lobes, while the upper lip has a central peak with soft winged curves ending at the corners of the mouth.

The ear is a cartilaginous shell, almost immovable. Elastic band muscles are situated behind the jaw at the bottom of the temporal and the edge of the zygomatic. The ear consists of an outer rim and an inner elevation. In front of it is the hollow with the opening of the canal and a small flap that blends into the side of the face. The lower part of the ear opening curves around and up into another smaller flap and below this hangs the lobe. The ear is vertically in line with the back of the jaw, and horizontally at the top it lines up between the

Illus. 63. Set down the main bone and muscle structure. Show the sterno-mastoid muscle in the neck; show the shoulder girdle.

line of the brow and the tip of the nose. Don't forget the mastoid bone in back of the ear shell.

Pay attention to the indentation above the chin, the sloping sides and the underpart. Note how the jaw line leads into the neck. Observe the round cylindrical shape of the throat.

Illus. 64. Use your tools to model the deltoids and the clavicles. Relate the muscles to the bones. Place the eyeballs in the sockets. Model around the outer areas.

Don't forget to indicate the sterno-mastoid muscles that originate from the bony prominences behind the ears and slant forward and down the side to the front clavicle and breast-bone—but don't accentuate them (Illustration 63). Note the line in back of the neck from under the back of the skull, down the center of the neck and into the middle of the upper back in between the shoulder blades (Illustration 61). Notice the subtle depressions and prominences of the diamond-shaped trapezius with apex well down the back.

Don't forget the triangular deltoid muscle, which gives form to the shoulder. This muscle is almost a perfect triangle. The apex goes down into the outer arm. The base goes up and around from the top shoulder blade to collarbone. Model it softly (Illustration 64).

In front be sure that you model the S-shaped collarbone where it depresses and then comes up forward and around. Note the high and low areas. Use your wire tools to establish large planes. Use your wood tools to make convex and concave curves across, up and down, in and out. Experiment. If there is too much clay in a particular spot, remove it with your tool; if there is not enough, add pellets of clay until you arrive at the amount sufficient to get the result you want. Use your thumbs. Co-ordinate your brain, eyes and hands (Illustrations 65 through 68).

The hair should be treated as a mass-form. Don't model each strand (Illustration 65). If you are doing a fairly literal portrait, keep the hair mass simple but make it contribute to the design. You will find something interesting in the natural growth direction of the hair itself. Don't make too deep shadow-forming undercuts. Don't ever do this where the hairline begins or it will look like a wig. Let the skin and hair blend together gently. Where you want to achieve the effect of light or sheen on the hair, treat it simply and smoothly.

If you have planned to do someone's portrait, make all

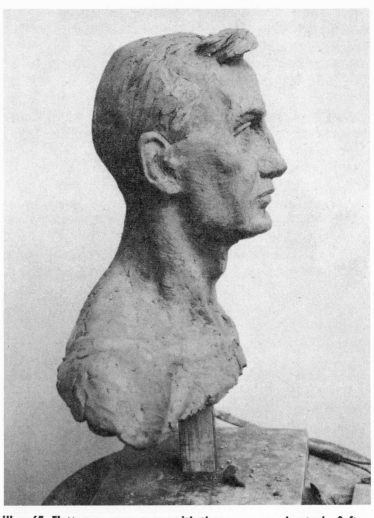

Illus. 65. Flatten or curve areas with the proper wooden tools. Soften one area into another, blending them together.

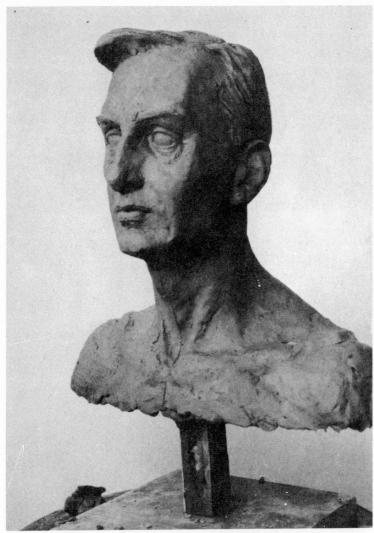

Illus. 66. Indent and build up where necessary. Use your fingers to model. Hollows are easily made with wire tools.

Illus. 67. Turn your model constantly and work on all parts. Look at it from above. It must be accurate from every view. The proportions must be correct. If they are not, add or subtract clay as needed.

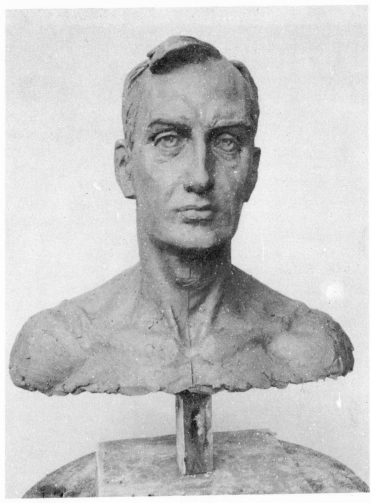

Illus. 68. With small wooden tools model the lids, nose, mouth and ears. Remember the bone structure beneath the muscles—it is still there.

the preparations before you have him sit for you. The clay should be worked and already massed on the armature. Make some preliminary pencil sketches. Take a number of snapshots all around, especially of the back and three-quarters. Don't let your sitter pose. Make him forget he is posing. Talk to him about anything. Put him at ease. And don't let him sit too long. Try to decide what are his chief or salient characteristics; make notes in a notebook. Is his head round, square, broad, long? Is his forehead receding or prominent? Is his skull highest at the front or toward the back? Does he have definite cheek bones? Has he deep eye sockets? Are his ears set low or high? Are his temples wider than his jaw? Does his profile curve convexly or concavely? Is his neck stringy, strong, weak, or straight?

Is your sitter a powerful, affirmative person or is he a mild, passive, pensive type? Classify him from the beginning and accent and concentrate on the forms that led you to your conclusions about him. Remember that sculpture begins with the inner structure.

9. Learning More About the Head

Now that you have attempted your first head or bust from life, you will undoubtedly have come to discover just how little you really know about the bones and muscles of the head. Now is a good time to add a bit of knowledge about such things.

THE BONES OF THE SKULL

Starting with the skull, think of it as an egg-shaped brain case or a rectangular box with a small rectangle attached, representing the maxillaries. It is, of course, neither, but a combination and modification of both of these geometric shapes. From above it is actually egg shaped; from the front it will vary from ovoid (egg), to square, to rectangular, depending on the skull you are copying (Illustrations 69–75).

Draw it first as an oval or egg shape. You can even start with a circle and then modify it. Draw it from above, then draw it from the front. Draw just the outline, don't try the detail yet. Now draw it in profile. After you have done this several times, draw the skull as a rectangular box with a smaller

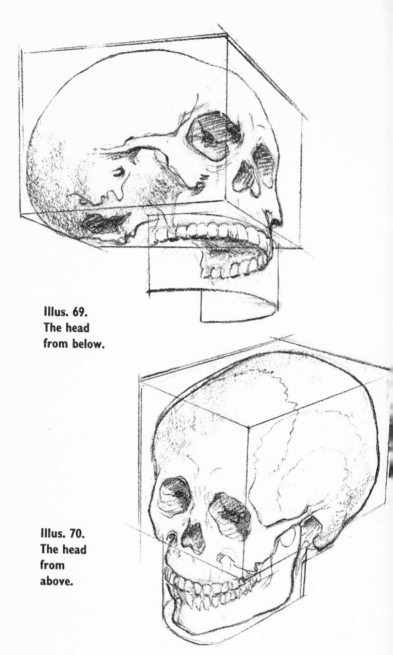

Illus. 69.
The head
from below.

Illus. 70.
The head
from
above.

one beneath it. Do it over until you have the general shape firmly in mind. Then try drawing it from memory (Illustrations 69 and 70).

Learn some of the names of the bones. It will give you a feeling of knowledge. The frontal bone is the forehead, the temporals are the bones on the sides of the skull, and the two parietal bones from the major part of the crown of the head. These have notched irregular seams (in a newborn child these seams are open, in the very old they are solidified). The two parietals meet each other at the top of the head and join the forehead (frontal) in front and the temporals on the sides and the occipital in back. The occipital bone forms the base of the skull in back. It is thick and strong. The spinal cord passes through an opening in its underside. The brain case (composed of all the bones mentioned above) rests on the first cervical vertebra, called "atlas," appropriately enough, because it supports the globe. A spiked bone from the second cervical vertebra is called the axis, also for a very obvious reason. It supplies flexible movements for the neck and acts as axis.

THE FACIAL BONES

The zygomatic arch rises on the side from the temple (temporal). It comes forward and becomes the malar or cheekbone, which also forms the lower edge of the eye socket. At the outer part, the zygomatic arch then joins into the frontal bone above the eye, which forms the upper edge of the socket (Illustration 72).

There is a small concave bone between the temporal and the frontal bone. This little bone is called the sphenoid.

The superior maxillary begins on the side of the nose, below the brow, flares out across and meets the cheekbone, then goes down and flattens in, meeting (and joining its counterpart) in the center below the nose, under the upper lip. The maxillaries form the upper arch, out of which the upper teeth grow.

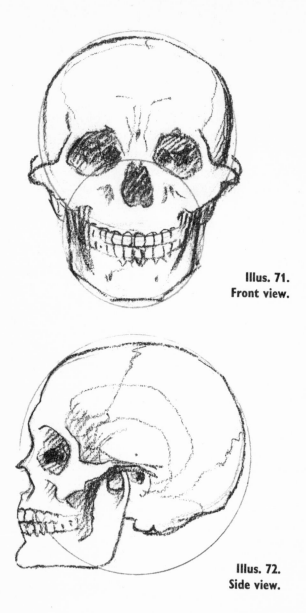

Illus. 71.
Front view.

Illus. 72.
Side view.

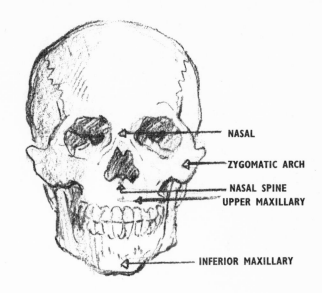

Illus. 73. Frontal bones labelled.

NASAL

ZYGOMATIC ARCH

NASAL SPINE
UPPER MAXILLARY

INFERIOR MAXILLARY

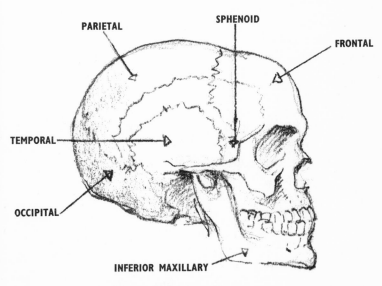

PARIETAL

SPHENOID

FRONTAL

TEMPORAL

OCCIPITAL

INFERIOR MAXILLARY

Illus. 74. Bones labelled, side view.

The nose is made up of two little bones which come together and are joined in the middle. They meet the brow at the top and extend down to form the bridge. The lower end of the nose is formed of cartilage.

The jawbone or the inferior maxillary is the only movable part of the head. It is shaped like a horseshoe. The posterior flat side of it forms almost a right angle with the lower arch of the jaw. It goes back and up and hinges under the zygomatic arch (Illustration 73).

So much for the basic bone structure of the head. This, of course, is only one-half of the story. On the foundation of the bones are laid the layers of muscles, cartilage and skin that complete the head.

THE MUSCLES OF THE HEAD AND NECK

Before closing this chapter here are a few pointers concerning the muscles of the head and neck which you will find very helpful. Remember that the strength of the neck is in the back. The neck comes up from the shoulders in the form of a cylinder curving slightly forward. The chin juts out over it in front like a canopy and the skull overhangs it in back. At the back of the neck there are groups of erector muscles which are covered over by the trapezius, and covered over on the sides by two big muscles called the sterno-mastoids. These muscles are two broad bands going from behind the ears to the front collarbone and breastbone. In front at each point of attachment, each muscle divides in two. One part attaches to the front clavicle and the other to the sternum.

Always remember to give fullness to the throat. This will denote both strength and youth. In a man, the Adam's apple is more pronounced. In a woman, it is smaller, but the thyroid is larger. A woman's throat should be modelled in a much smoother, much rounder way. Never make the sterno-mastoid muscle stand out or stringy looking, as most beginners do.

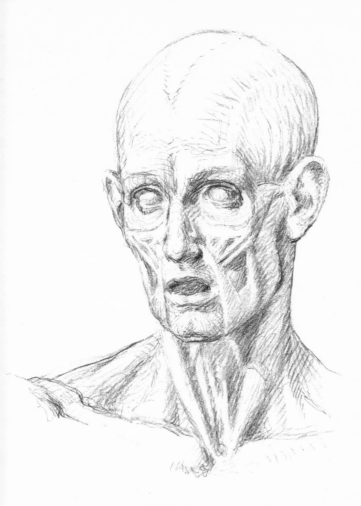

Illus. 75. Head showing muscles.

Notice that the front of the throat forms a triangle with the base at the under back of the chin.

A fibrous sheath called the platysma goes from the lower cheek and jaw over the sides of the neck and clavicle, where it joins with the deltoid and the chest muscles. This skin muscle draws down the corners of the mouth and lifts the skin of the neck into high folds.

Over the head like a close-fitting cap is an "inner skin." This ends, and is attached at two points, at the back of the skull. This inner skin cap ends on the forehead in two frontal muscles, which function to raise the eyebrows and also pull the "cap" forward. The muscles of the temple converge and come forward and under the zygomatic arch. In the back of the cheekbone they attach to the lower jaw.

Under the frontal muscles, above the top of the nose, are two frowning muscles. Frown at yourself in the mirror and you will see them quite plainly. There are even a number of muscles on the nose itself. And on either side of the nose two thin strips go down to the "ring muscled" mouth. These pull up the lip and nostrils. Two more strips pass down the cheeks to the outer upper lip. These pull the corners of the mouth up and out.

Complete circles of muscle fibres surround the eyes. These flattened rings spread up over the frontal eye socket and down on the cheekbones. They separate in the middle and form the upper and lower lids.

The "ring muscle" of the mouth is more elastic than that of the "eye rings." This is because the mouth is a sphincter muscle and the eye muscles are not. From the back angle of the jaw directly forward to the corners of the mouth are the muscles which pull the mouth out sideways. These are called buccinators, covered over somewhat by the zygomatic strips of muscles but principally covered over by the strongest and largest face muscles called the masseters or chewing muscles. From the lower part of the cheekbone these large muscles come down over the back angle of the jaw; along the back edge, down and around, and then toward the chin.

Further in on each side of the chin are muscles extending from the lower lip down to form each side of the chin. Lastly, there are two wedge-shaped muscles that make up the front part of the chin. The underpart of the chin is made up of various muscles that go towards the hyoid bone in the throat and help in swallowing and opening the jaw.

There are no muscles in the ears and lower part of the nose—these consist of cartilage. The surrounding muscles may afford them some limited movements.

The shapes and forms of the muscles of the face vary with the individual personality and the degree of development of the muscles themselves (Illustration 75). Therefore, the human face cannot really be described because of the infinite varieties presented, not only by the number of possible form combinations but by the uniqueness of each individual.

10. Learning the Anatomy of the Body

As you have learned in the chapter on the anatomy of the head, there is no need to study anatomy in great detail. Nor must you study it systematically in quite the same way a surgeon does. But there is, however, a need to learn the proportions and the basic bony and muscular parts of the human body. In order to draw or model a figure in any position, you must become thoroughly familiar with its construction. The study of anatomy will help you to understand not only the human form but also its infinite movements and balances. These are most desirable and most difficult to attain in sculpture. Action requires knowledge of the figure, plus the laws of gravity, plus design, in order to bring into being a creation flowing with rhythmic beauty.

THE VERTEBRAE

To clarify the structure of the 24 vertebrae, these can be divided into three sections: the 7 vertebrae of the neck, called the cervicals; the middle section to which the ribs are attached are the 12 dorsals; and the lower 5 vertebrae of the spinal

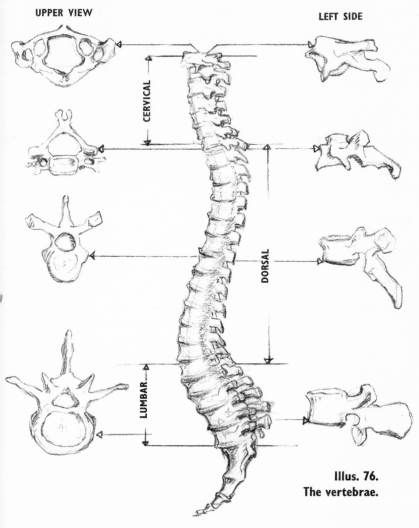

CERVICAL

DORSAL

LUMBAR

Illus. 76.
The vertebrae.

column are the lumbar vertebrae. These last are the strongest. The dorsals are adapted for ribs and the cervicals, the smallest, are the most flexible.

The spine looks straight when you view it from the back

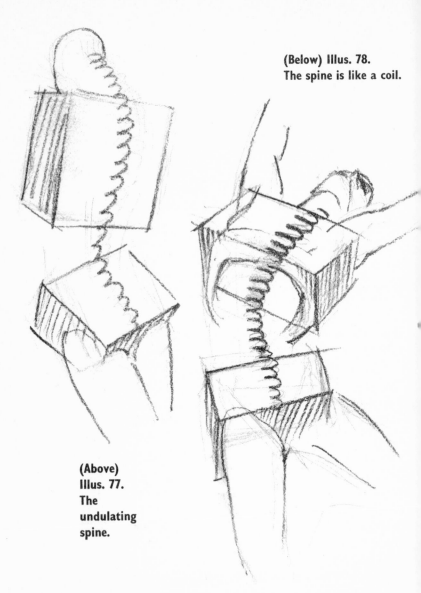

(Below) Illus. 78.
The spine is like a coil.

(Above)
Illus. 77.
The
undulating
spine.

or the front. But it really is not straight at all when you look at it from the side. From the head it curves out to the shoulders,

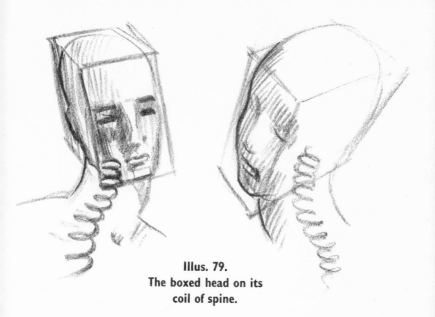

Illus. 79.
The boxed head on its
coil of spine.

then in along the dorsal and out again at the lower end (Illustration 76).

This undulating line is man's lifeline, a flexible chain that makes it possible for him to stand upright and to balance and bend in innumerable ways. The clearest illustration of the amazing flexibility of the spine, is to visualize the fixed boxes of the skull, thorax (chest) and pelvis joined together by this undulating chain of ingenious vertebrae (Illustration 77). The body is able to assume the most exaggerated positions, far removed from the straight, central, perpendicular, only because of the supple elasticity afforded by the spinal column.

Draw the head with the neck, i.e., with the seven cervicals. Draw it simply. Draw it with the head bent forward, with the head sideways, with it bent backwards. Draw just a springy-looking coil for the neck (Illustration 79). Put movement into the head on the top, as it would bend, bow and turn if it were actually on the top of a flexible coil. Now add the thorax or

85

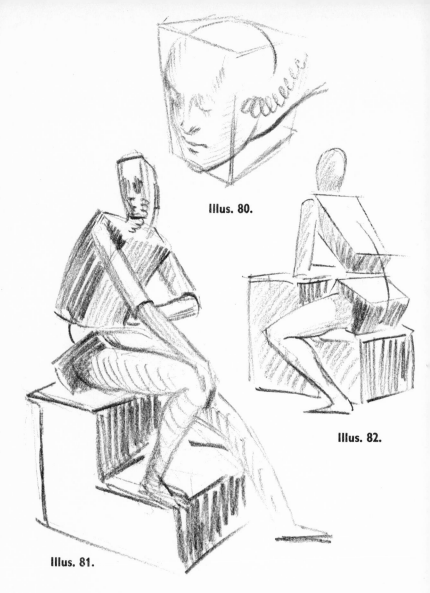

Illus. 80.

Illus. 82.

Illus. 81.

rib cage. Draw it very simply, like a box. Show the spinal bones as a continuing coil. Sketch in the attached ribs. Add the box of the pelvis. Hang it on a curved coil of lumbar vertebrae (Illustrations 77 through 85).

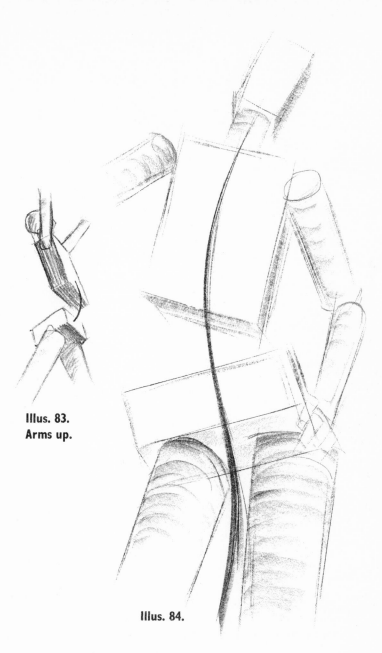

Illus. 83.
Arms up.

Illus. 84.

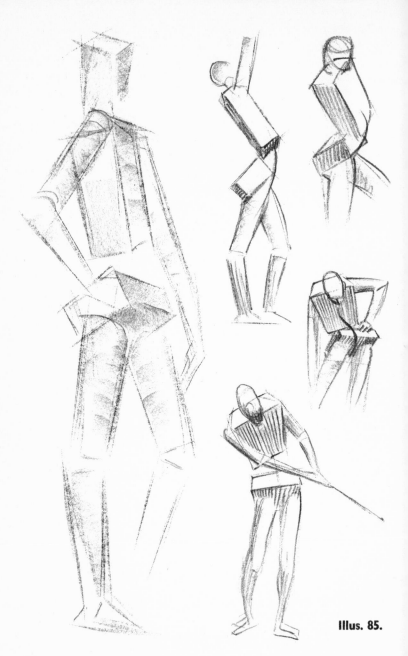

Illus. 85.

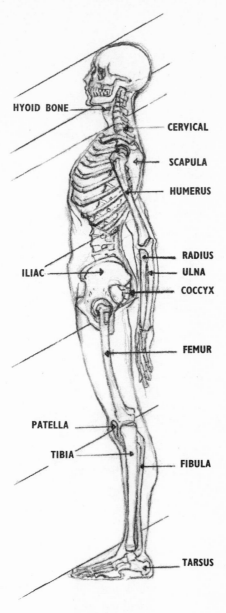

HYOID BONE

CERVICAL

SCAPULA

HUMERUS

RADIUS

ULNA

COCCYX

ILIAC

FEMUR

PATELLA

TIBIA

FIBULA

TARSUS

Illus. 86. Bones.

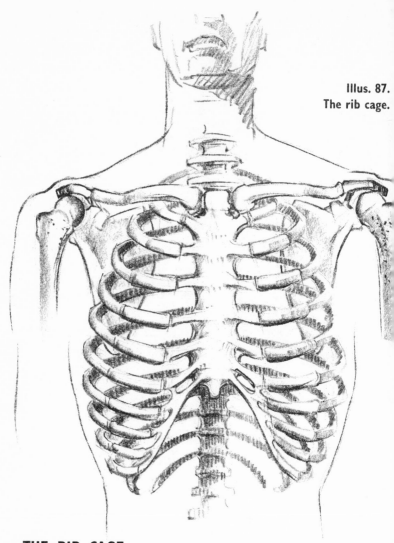

THE RIB CAGE

Notice that the rib cage is not rigid—it expands with every breath. Its structure is yielding, and it is actually narrower at the top and wider at the bottom. From the side view it slants down diagonally to the front. Also note that at the bottom, the eleventh and twelfth ribs are short and free. They do not come around to the front of the body. All the others do and are attached to the breastbone (sternum). The sternum is often referred to as a Roman sword. The hilt or uppermost part ends at the pit of the neck. The middle part has been called the blade and the lower is the point (Illustration 87).

THE SHOULDER GIRDLE

In front, at the top of the rib cage over the first two ribs, are the clavicles—one on each side, horizontally between the

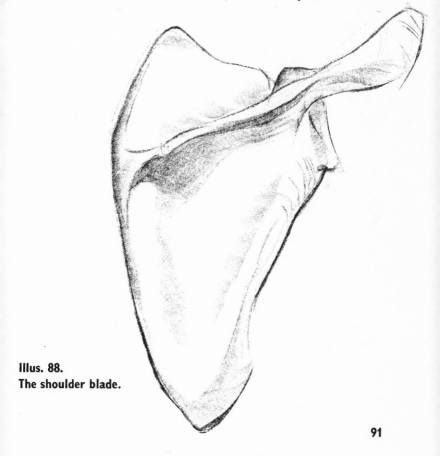

Illus. 88.
The shoulder blade.

hilt of the breastbone and the knobs of the shoulder blades. The clavicles together with the shoulder blades (scapulae) form what is known as the shoulder girdle and encircle the top of the chest. The collarbones are quite movable, as you can prove by moving your shoulders up and down, back and forth, twisting and turning and tilting, quite independently of the chest. The shoulder blades are flat triangular bones, their outer high ridge knobs are known as the acromion processes. These outside shoulder knobs are joined by the clavicles to form the outermost points of the shoulder girdle. Under these outer ends of joined clavicles and acromion processes are the sockets in the shoulder blades, into which the upper ends of the arms are fitted (Illustration 87).

THE ARM BONES

The upper arm bone is called the humerus. This is a ball and socket joint, lubricated, braced, and properly bound for optimum movement by ligaments and tendons. The upper arm bone ends at the elbow in two projections known as the inner and outer condyles—the two little knobs on each side of your funny bone. Between these two is a smooth spool-like surface, this is grasped by a bone in the forearm (ulna) which is notched to fit. The elbow is a hinged joint. Bend your elbow, extend it, feel the motion, the action.

The other bone in the forearm is the radius. The radius starts from the thumb side of the hand, while the ulna is on the little finger side. The radius crosses the ulna in certain positions when you turn your hands (Illustration 90). Try it. Turn your palms up, now down. Feel the bones twist?

The wrist is attached to the hand and moves with it and as part of it. It is made up of eight, almost-square, little bones, known as the carpal bones. Rotate your hand and you can readily see that the wrist forms part of the joint and makes movement quite easy.

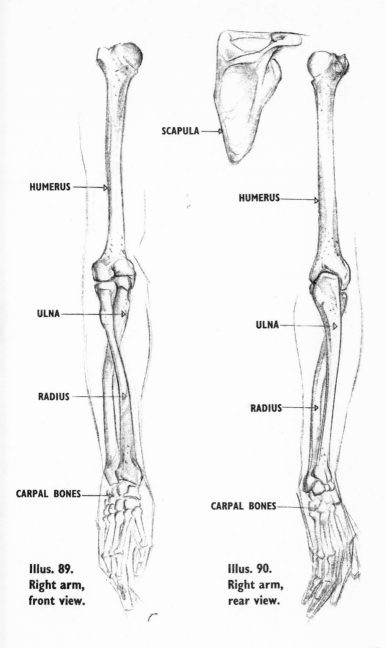

SCAPULA

HUMERUS

HUMERUS

ULNA

ULNA

RADIUS

RADIUS

CARPAL BONES

CARPAL BONES

Illus. 89.
Right arm,
front view.

Illus. 90.
Right arm,
rear view.

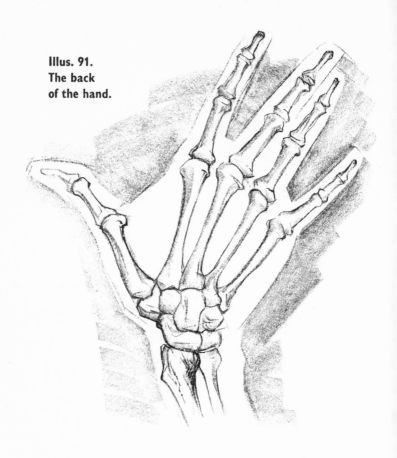

**Illus. 91.
The back
of the hand.**

Notice that the hand as a mass is less heavy on the little finger side, than it is on the thumb side. Also notice that the palm of the hand is longer than the back. The back of the hand is flat when you make a fist. Compare the length of the thumb with that of the middle finger. Observe that the thumb is shorter and stronger and opposes the other fingers. It does not lie parallel but at an angle. Compare the length and joints of each finger.

The construction of the hand should be given some study and attention (Illustration 91). You will find later on that hands are very important in sculpture. They are extremely expressive and many sculptors believe they are even more so than the face.

THE PELVIC AREA

Let us go back now to have another look at the vertebrae. You have already seen that the chest and the pelvis can be visualized as boxes on a strip of flexible spine, but notice that the lower end of this chain of vertebrae is solidified into a wedge-shaped single bone known as the sacrum (Illustration 92). At the tip of the sacrum are three or four small bones called the coccyx, which seems to be all that is left of a tail in man.

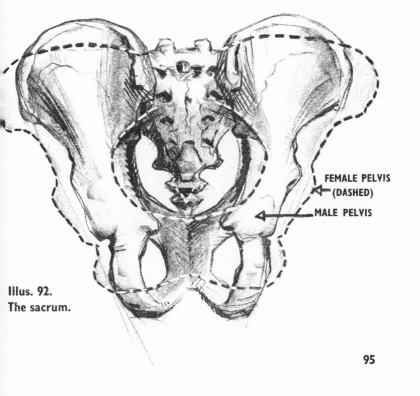

FEMALE PELVIS
(DASHED)

MALE PELVIS

Illus. 92.
The sacrum.

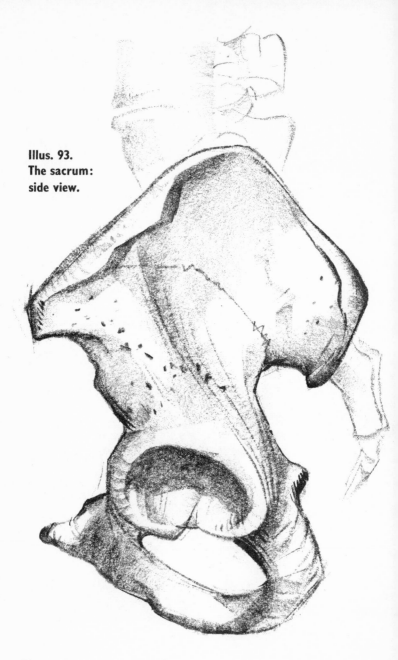

Illus. 93.
The sacrum:
side view.

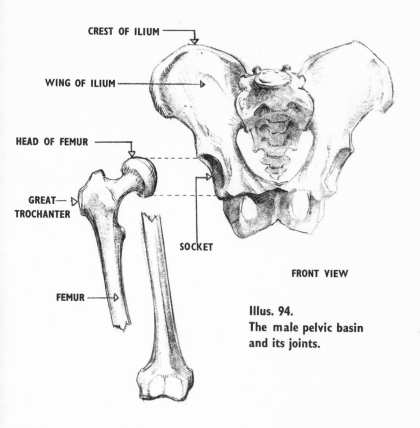

CREST OF ILIUM

WING OF ILIUM

HEAD OF FEMUR

GREAT—
TROCHANTER

SOCKET

FRONT VIEW

FEMUR

Illus. 94.
The male pelvic basin
and its joints.

The sacrum and the pelvis are joined together. From the sacrum (lower spine) curving around on both sides to the front are two wing-shaped bones which constitute the pelvic basin. These wing bones make up the ilium, which consists of (1) the upper crest, (2) the middle or outer, which contains the thighbone socket, and (3) the lower, which comes forward to form the bone known as the symphysis pubis. The lowest part of the ilium (ischium), contains two hollow rings, on which the body rests when in a sitting position.

Remember that the female pelvis is deeper from front to back than the male's. It is also wider and shorter.

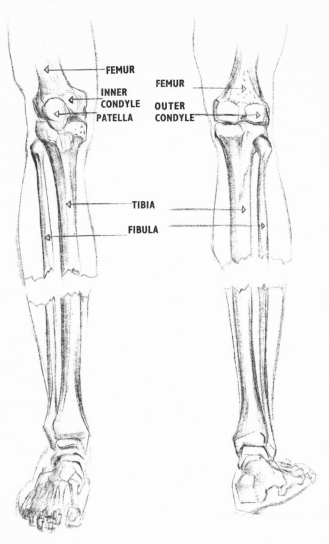

FEMUR

INNER
CONDYLE

PATELLA

FEMUR

OUTER
CONDYLE

TIBIA

FIBULA

Illus. 95. Tibia and fibula. (Left) Right leg, front view. (Right) Right leg, rear view.

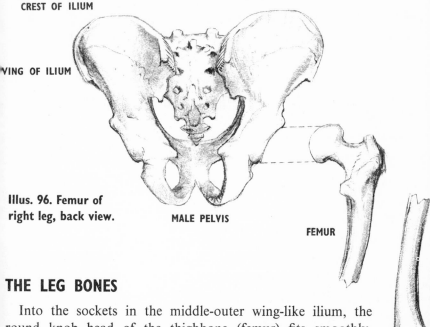

CREST OF ILIUM

VING OF ILIUM

Illus. 96. Femur of
right leg, back view.

MALE PELVIS

FEMUR

THE LEG BONES

Into the sockets in the middle-outer wing-like ilium, the round knob head of the thighbone (femur) fits smoothly. Connecting this head with the shaft is a neck-shaped bone that goes out, down and back, and ends in a protuberance called the great trochanter (Illustration 96). This defines the widest part of the hips. Below it and on the back of the shaft is a smaller protuberance, which is the lesser trochanter. Notice that the thighbone is not a straight bone but it curves forward, then slightly back, and then proceeds down towards the knee, ending in two condyles that lie on the head of the lower leg bone (tibia) (Illustration 95). The femur is the longest bone in the human body.

The leg, as you can readily see by bending your knee, flexes backwards, while we have already seen that the arm bends forward at the elbow. Whereas the elbow has extreme flexibility built into its structure, the knee has strength. The knee's function is flexion and extension (bending and unbending).

Unlike the two bones (ulna and radius) of the forearm, the two bones in the lower leg (tibia and fibula) do not cross each other. Nor do they divide the work between them as do the forearm bones. Instead, the tibia, which is the sturdier bone in the leg, does all the work and the fibula serves as a kind of anchor for attaching muscles (Illustration 95).

The knee cap (patella), is a round little bone on the front of the knee. It is attached by a ligament to the strong tibia bone in the lower leg. The knee cap moves with this bone. It moves smoothly over the hollow between the two condyles of the thighbone. Bend your knee and you will be able to see and feel the flattish round kneecap. Bend your knee back and forth, on each side of the cap you can feel and see the smooth action of the articulating condyles of the thigh bone (femur) as they come forward and rest on the top of the sturdy tibia. The shaft of the tibia should curve slightly; if it curved too much you would look bowlegged. The lower part of the tibia ends in a knobby head. The inner part of it forms the inside ankle bone. The two bones in the lower leg are the same length; but the fibula, which is the bone on the outside of the tibia, doesn't enter the knee joint but comes down lower. At the end it forms the outside of the ankle. It is lower than the inside part of the ankle and more towards the back. Remember, never represent the ankle bones on the same level. The two lower leg bones (tibia and fibula) are fastened together, above and below. There is no rolling movement like the forearm, but there is a limited gliding movement.

THE FOOT

Between the leg and the foot (giving elasticity to the joint) is the tarsus. The tarsus is made up of seven little bones in contrast to the eight in the wrist. And, unlike the wrist bones, they are not squarish nor are they arranged in rows. Of these seven bones that make up the tarsus, the two most important

Illus. 97.

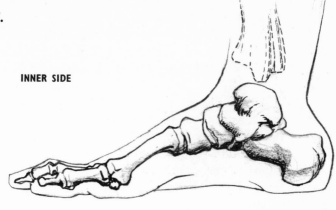

INNER SIDE

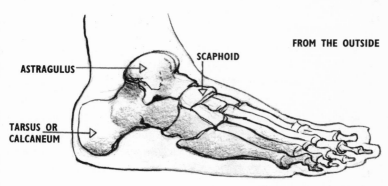

FROM THE OUTSIDE

ASTRAGULUS

SCAPHOID

TARSUS OR
CALCANEUM

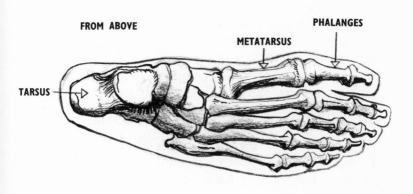

FROM ABOVE

METATARSUS

PHALANGES

TARSUS

include the saddle-shaped bone called the astragalus in front (on this the sturdy tibia leg bone ends and slides back and forth and rests) and the heel bone. This latter bone makes up the outer and back part of the foot, while the saddle-shaped bone is more to the inner side. These two bones do not lie above each other. The underside of the saddle bone rests on the forward part of the heel bone. The rest of the heel bone goes back and down. Notice that the length of the foot goes back quite far behind the ankle (Illustration 97).

After the saddle-shaped (astragalus) bone and the heel bone (calcaneum), the next bone in importance is the scaphoid. This bone forms the higher, inner point of the instep. Located between the heel bone, the saddle-shaped bone, and the high instep bone are four smaller bones that make a kind of bridge or arch. When you walk, these bones never touch the ground. Beyond the instep and before you come to the toes, are five bones, one for the support of each toe (metatarsus). These are longer and stronger than the metacarpals in the hand. If you wiggle your toes and touch your foot at the same time, you can feel each metatarsus above each toe. The phalanges make up the toes, and they are joined to the metatarsals. The phalanges of the toes are shorter than those in the fingers and thumbs; and they are smaller and thinner with the exception of the big toe. This toe, like the thumb, lacks a phalange. Its tip turns up. And though it is separated from the other toes, it is not thrust out at an extreme angle like the thumb. Look at your toes, look at your feet and ankles. Make studies of them. Wet the underside of your feet and step on a piece of brown paper. Notice the impressions. The outer edges of the feet leave a mark, the inner arches do not.

THE MUSCLES OF THE TRUNK AND LIMBS

While you have seen how marvelously constructed man's skeleton is and how perfectly placed the bones are, you must have also realized that bones alone have no movement by

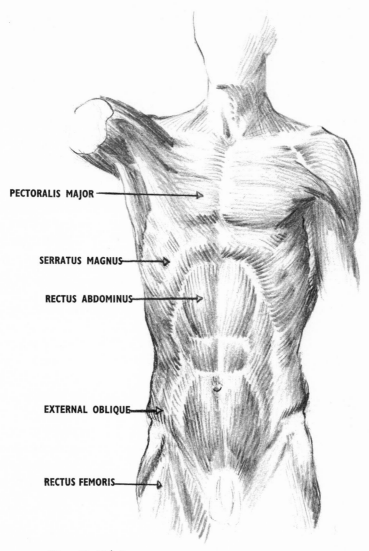

PECTORALIS MAJOR

SERRATUS MAGNUS

RECTUS ABDOMINUS

EXTERNAL OBLIQUE

RECTUS FEMORIS

Illus. 98. The front muscles.

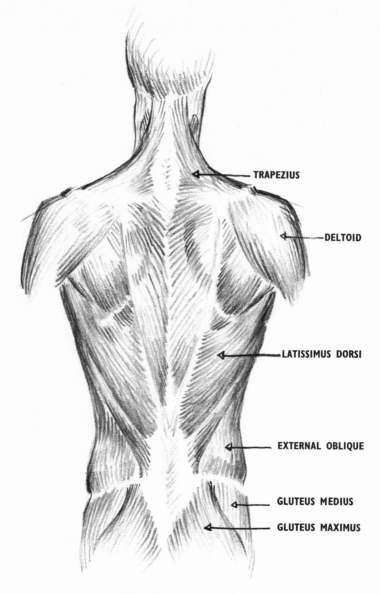

TRAPEZIUS

DELTOID

LATISSIMUS DORSI

EXTERNAL OBLIQUE

GLUTEUS MEDIUS

GLUTEUS MAXIMUS

Illus. 99. The back muscles.

themselves. Bones need muscles. And when directed by brain and nerves, muscles give action and power. They expand and contract and move the skeleton. Muscles go in pairs. For every muscle which by contraction pulls a bone in one direction there is another muscle that can pull it in the opposite direction. Every muscle is engineered to do a special job of its own. The muscular structure of the body is designed with elements of contrast and symmetry, variety and repetition. The decorative forms are extraordinarily beautiful. Copy these muscle patterns and see for yourself how truly remarkable they are. They will reveal to you all the basic plane geometric forms and modifications: triangle, rectangle, square, oval, etc., and their relationship to the basic 3-dimensional shapes—the cube, the cone, the sphere, the cylinder. You will be convinced that you are wonderfully made.

THE ABDOMINAL MUSCLES

On either side of the spine from the tip of the sacrum all the way up to the base of the skull, is a group of twin muscles. They are thickest at the small of the back—further up they thin out and spread. At the neck they become closer and up further divide and enter the bones of the neck and the base of the skull. Because these muscles serve to hold the body erect, they are called erectors. On the opposite side, or front, of the body and acting in opposition to the erector muscles are the rectus abdominus muscles. From the lower abdomen these muscles go up over the abdomen to the breastbone and the seventh ribs, where they are attached. Where these muscles cover the soft part of the body in front, they are re-inforced by and divided into four groups of muscles: the largest is from the navel to the symphysis. This linea alba (white line) marks the midline of the body in front and corresponds to the spine in the back. A white, flat elastic sheath on each side of the abdominal muscle goes down on each side past the groin to the symphysis (Illustration 98).

THE MUSCLES OF THE BACK, SHOULDERS & NECK

Just over the iliac crest, two external oblique muscles begin. They go diagonally up, out and back over the lower ribs and round the side of the body. The upper part of the obliques divide into strips and intertwine with others that come around from the back of the body. These muscles pull diagonally because they are placed on the bias. They turn, twist and pull the rib cage down. Again there are two large muscles (dorsi) on the back which oppose these obliques. The muscles under the armpits dovetail with the obliques and are called the serratus magnus muscles. You can only see the ends of them under the armpit; but they come from the underpart of the shoulder blades. Between the blades and the rib cage they divide into fingerlike sections, each one attached to a rib. Their function is to pull the shoulder blades forward and down. You cannot see much of them because they are under the shoulder blades by the dorsi muscles, the big muscles on the back which oppose the obliques. The dorsi muscles begin all the way down on the back at the sacrum. They begin as a white flat tendon, cover the lumbar, come up the middle of the back, then get thicker on each side of the midline. Coming up diagonally, they twist around and under the arm (Illustration 99).

Just as dorsi muscles oppose the external obliques, the serratus magnus muscles are opposed by the rhomboids. The rhomboids draw the shoulder blades up and back again, while as you have already seen, the serratus draws them down and forward. The rhomboids are almost covered over by other muscles, but it is a broad muscle and extends from the fourth vertebra in the back of the neck to the fourth dorsal vertebra.

Still another muscle of the shoulders, neck and back is the trapezius. This begins at the base of the skull, spreads over the shoulders to the upper-outer crest of the blades and clavicle. It extends down the middle of the back in a V shape.

The opposing muscles on the front of the body are the pectoral, or chest, muscles. They rise from the inner part of the collarbone, down along the breastbone, over the chest to the arms. Slanting from above down and from below upward, forming two sides of a triangle, they overlap other muscles and end at the upper arm.

THE ARM MUSCLES

The deltoid muscle that covers the upper outer arm and shoulder goes from the outer shoulder around the outermost acromion process and around in front to the collarbone. It serves to raise the arm sideways. It is the large upper muscle on the outside of your arm. If you raise your arm to shoulder level you can feel this large deltoid muscle as a padded lump. In this position you will also note quite an indentation or deep dimple at the joint where the collarbone and scapula meet at the outermost point of your shoulder. In front, the deltoid meets the upper edge of the chest muscles. The deltoid perfoms the simple and direct action of pulling from shoulder girdle to arm. It joins the arm and body muscles. Muscles, of course, always go from anchor points on one bone to another; otherwise, you would never have any action at all.

Underneath the biceps on the long shaft bone (humerus) of the arm you have two smaller muscles, one that bridges the gap between the biceps and the chest muscles (coraco-bracialis) and which helps to draw the arm forward and down and opposes the deltoid. The other small muscle (bracialis anticus) is broader halfway down the shaft, passes over the front of the elbow and goes into the upper forearm (ulna). The biceps lie over both of these muscles, and begin from under the deltoids. Limb muscles taper and become white tendons, tying into the bone structure, and so do the biceps. They are attached to the shoulder girdle above the arm joint. This attachment ensures not only the flexing of the forearm, but the ability to draw the arm up and forward, as in chinning (Illustration 100).

In the forearm you will find five groups of muscles that perform different functions. The pronators, supinators, extensors, flexors, and special extensors. These are all involved in pulling, turning, twisting (pronators and supinators), extending and flexing. The flexors on the inner smooth side oppose the extensors on the outer forearm.

The thumb has special extensors. These muscles cross over diagonally from the radius and come between the tendons of the extensors. Two of them continue as tendons on the inner side of the wrist down to the thumb.

In the palm of the hand you will notice large flexors, while the back of the hand has an interlacing of small muscles between the bones. Look at your own hands. Make sketches and drawings of them in various postions. Model them in clay. You will find this both interesting and delightful. Hands are very expressive—supplicating, prayerful, to grasping, helpless, or delicate. See how much and how many different emotions you can put into your hands.

THE LEG MUSCLES

You should also know something about the rest of the body's muscular construction. The hip muscles are of course the largest and strongest. These form the buttocks (gluteus maximus). In front of the gluteus maximus and on the side of the hips straight down from the middle of the iliac crest are the gluteus medius muscles. The function of these muscles is to draw the thighs out sideways away from each other. The third hip muscle is the tensor of the thigh fascia. It is the smallest one, narrower than the other two and shorter. In front of the hip bone (trochanter) it becomes a sheath, merges with the gluteus maximus, passes down the outer side of the

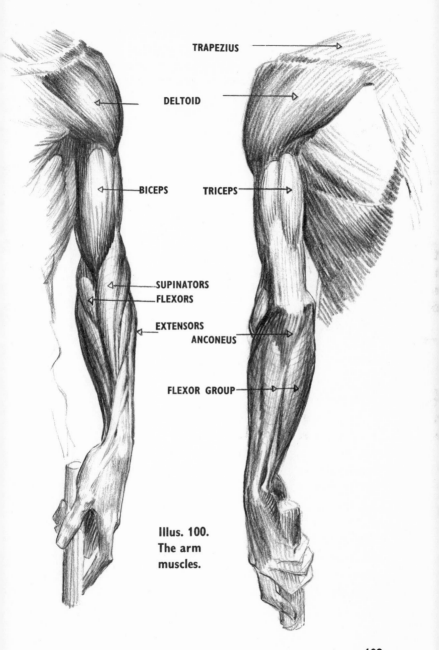

TRAPEZIUS

DELTOID

BICEPS   TRICEPS

SUPINATORS

FLEXORS

EXTENSORS

ANCONEUS

FLEXOR GROUP

Illus. 100.
The arm
muscles.

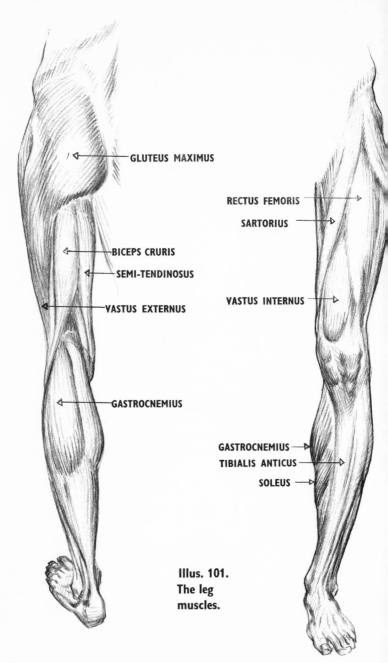

GLUTEUS MAXIMUS

RECTUS FEMORIS

SARTORIUS

BICEPS CRURIS

SEMI-TENDINOSUS

VASTUS EXTERNUS

VASTUS INTERNUS

GASTROCNEMIUS

GASTROCNEMIUS

TIBIALIS ANTICUS

SOLEUS

Illus. 101.
The leg
muscles.

110

thigh, and ends below the knee joint in the head of the shinbone (tibia). This muscle helps to flex the thigh (Illustration 101).

A number of muscles along the inner side of the thighbone are known as the adductor muscles. One of them goes down, and its tendon continues to the inner side of the head of the lower leg bone (gracilis).

Two large muscles lie on the front of the thigh. The vastus externus goes down to just above the knee and is attached to the kneecap as a tendon. It serves to extend and rotate the leg outward. The vastus internus goes over the thighbone (femur) toward the inner side and attaches to the kneecap at a lower level than the externus. The vastus internus extends and rotates the leg inward.

The sartorius muscle is like an S-shaped ribbon. It goes from the ilium down, then in, then forward again into the lower leg shaft (tibia). This muscle is the longest muscle in the human body and rotates the thigh out and in.

Meeting in the center of the back of the thigh are twin muscles the biceps cruris and the semi-tendinosus and semi-membranosus. These last two serve to flex the knee and rotate the leg inward. The biceps cruris are flexor muscles and lie atop each other as do the other muscles in this group. Both groups narrow into tendons at the back of the knee. They form the inner and outer hamstrings. These four muscles function to flex the leg on the thigh.

Something important to note and to remember is that the hip socket, the knee and the ankle are all in line. This will help you later when you model a figure.

The knee itself has no muscles at all. It is more or less cube shaped. Between the bone and the skin there are only tendons and ligaments. The thigh extensors stop before they reach the knee and the muscles of the leg begin below the head of the tibia (the sturdy lower leg bone). The tibia anticus arises at the front outer shaft, goes in and down along the bone and becomes a tendon. Then it goes down under a ligament and into the inside of the instep (metatarsal). Its function, of course, is to pull the foot up and in. Right beside the tibialis is the common extensor of the toes. Halfway down, this too becomes tendinous, and under the annular ligament divides into four, one for each of the toes. The special extensor for the big toe appears between the tibialis and the common extensor. Just in front of the outer ankle is an extensor of the little toe.

Make a trip to your local art museum. Look at other sculptors' efforts at expression. Study how they solved proportions, balance, weight distribution. Notice the emphasis on the sturdy lower leg bone (tibia) in the stance.

On the outer side of the lower leg are the long and short peroneal muscles. These lie atop each other as the biceps cruris on the back of the thigh. The long peroneus becomes tendinous halfway down, while the short peroneus extends lower down as a muscle and becomes a tendon above the ankle. It then goes behind the ankle, then forward and inserts into the fifth bone of the metatarsus. The long peroneal tendon twists in and under the foot and over the instep and then into the first bone of the metatarsus.

Under the calf muscles at the back of the leg, attached near the top of the tibia and the fibula are tendons called the long flexors, which go down the tibia and the inside of the heel. A second tendon goes under the instep and divides into four parts, one for each of the smaller toes. Over the flexors is the soleus, flat and broad. On top of it and covering the upper part is the calf muscle (gastrocnemius). Together these go down into the powerful Achilles' tendon at the back of the lower leg, which in turn goes into the heel.

There are many muscle groups on the underpart of the foot but when you model it, pay more attention to the bony structure. Remember that on the inner side of the foot only the ball and heel touch the floor. The arch comes up definitely and the outside edge of the foot must be firmly planted on the ground. Take a look at your own foot. Wiggle your toes, rotate your ankle, and feel the tendons, bones and muscles involved in the movements. Learn to observe the high points and the low points in structure. Make sketches. Draw from different angles—from the sides, back, under. Use a mirror to get clearer and more varied views. You will find a full-length mirror a most remarkable aid. You will even become your own best model, learning and acquiring insight at your own pace.

Illus. 102. Prepare your armature: a simple board with an upright in the middle. At each end of two wires tie butterflies (two crossed pieces of wood). Have your clay already worked into sausage-shaped lengths.

11. Making a Torso

If you are going to make a torso, again start with an armature. Since very little of arms and legs are involved here, all you need is a sturdy twelve-inch-square board and a foot-long piece of ⅜″ pipe attached to a flange screwed to the center of the board. Attach two butterflies (small crossed pieces of wood) at each end of a wire and wind the wire around the top of the pipe. The butterflies hang halfway down and will keep the clay from slipping off (Illustration 102).

When you are modelling a torso, begin with the pelvis. Make a block with the clay tools and place it somewhat forward and slanting to one side. The leg bearing the weight of the body will push up that side of the pelvis. The rib box or thoracic cage is also shaped like a block made up of clay rolls and should be placed above the pelvis, but leaving a space between. (The space between is the lumbar region.) The rib cage is placed at an opposite or counter position to the slant of the pelvis. This not only gives the figure balance, but also movement and the very desirable, aesthetic S-line of beauty (Illustration 103).

In between the thorax and the pelvis, the soft abdominal mass is filled in at the front and the lumbar region at the

Illus. 103. Put your clay on to your armature. Make an upper and lower block. Counterbalance them. Use your wooden tools. With a knife, make the edges straight.

back (Illustration 104). Once you have established the large planes, then proceed to break them down into smaller ones.

Never lose sight of the middle lines of pelvis, thorax and neck.

Illus. 104. Add a smaller round block between the two large blocks. On the top of the upper block add a cylindrical form in the middle, for the neck.

One block counters the other. The linea alba in front must correspond with the spinal column in back. Model the soft area around the navel and above. Do not dig into the sternum. The

Illus. 105. Add parts of arms and legs. Determine the central axial line (linea alba).

rib cage is round. The breasts do not lie on a flat surface. They are as full above the nipple as they are below. They point outward, away from each other, not forward. Lines drawn from

Illus. 106. Remove some clay to show the joining points of neck and arms. Outline the abdominal arch. Place the pit of the neck, and the navel.

their points meet at the pit of the neck, forming a triangle. The pectoral muscles lie under the breasts and lift them when the arms are lifted. In this position, the breasts will point upward

Illus. 107. Add breasts. Fill in abdominal and lumbar regions. Use
your tools. Use your thumbs.

outward. Pay attention to the arch formed by the edge of the rib cage. Delineate the breastbone and the ribs. The front of the torso is symmetrically divided in halves by a vertical central groove—from the pit of the neck to the end of the breastbone, from the end of the breastbone to the navel and from the navel to the mound of the symphysis (Illustration 109). These four points divide the torso central line into equal thirds.

Do not make the waist too slim. In sculpture this would give the torso an undesirable frailty. The proportions, the movement, the balance, and—above all—the modelling, showing knowledge of bone underneath and muscle over, are your paramount aims at this time. As a beginner, you must establish basic essentials by doing a torso accurately and realistically. As you become conversant and expert in your visual and tactile sense development, you may want to do a portrait bust or torso in an interpretative way, eliminating or adding to the realistic. This requires quite an education sculpturally, since you must know what to eliminate, what to accentuate, and what to add.

In the beginning it is best to do a simple torso in a simple pose. In clay modelling as in every other endeavor it is best to take one step at a time and be successful at as many stages as possible. This will build up your confidence and lead you steadily on to more complex and involved poses and compositions.

When you have accomplished a satisfactory clay model of a torso you may want to do a full figure. This, of course, will require a different armature because of the arms and legs. Don't make the figure too big. A large figure may be a problem afterwards if you expect to do your own casting. If you can afford to employ an expert plaster caster, however, this will not be a problem. We strongly suggest that you make a figure about thirty inches tall at the beginning. Most professional sculptors start by doing small-scale figures and then work up

Illus. 108. Join the upper block smoothly into the middle section. Establish the abdominal planes.

to full-scale measurements. This is a wise procedure, for it affords the opportunity for any changes or solutions to any problems in the small model at the beginning when they can be easily and readily done.

Illus. 109. Soften and model one area into another. Work all round, all sides. Determine the symphysis. Resolve the thighs.

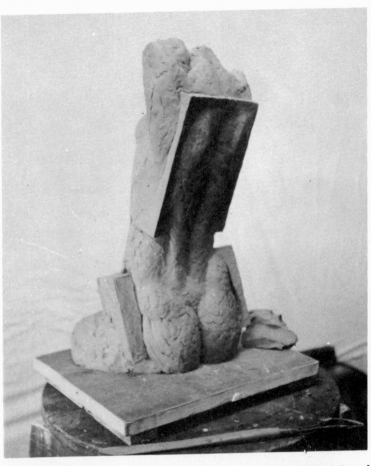

Illus. 110. Make sure you have the spine line well indicated and matching the front line. The masses on each side of these lines must be equal.

Illus. 111. Note that the back of the neck rises up from and is a continuation of the large diamond-shaped trapezius muscle.

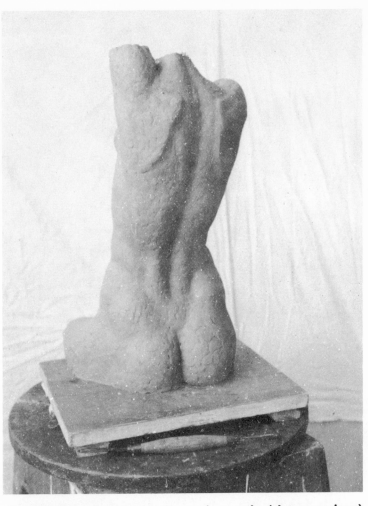

Illus. 112. Model the buttocks, the massive muscles (gluteus maximus), and the minor side hip muscles. Show where the indentation of the spine ends in a triangular form. Show the shoulder blades.

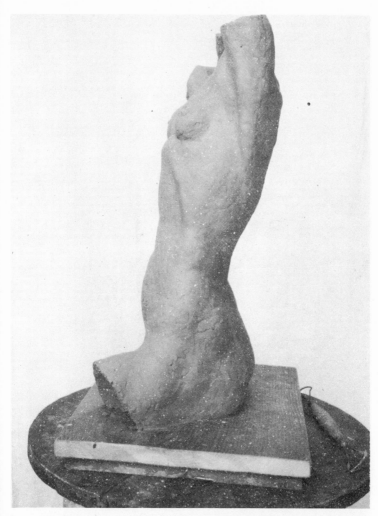

Illus. 113. Show the relationship of breast to armpit to edge of shoulder blade. In profile, show the ins and outs flowing gently from one area to the other, making a composed unit.

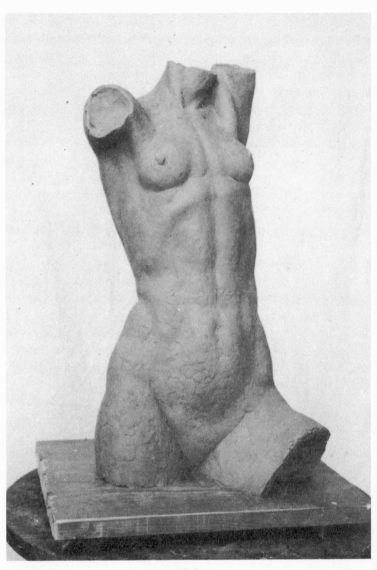

Illus. 114.

When you plan a single standing figure, you must give consideration to the legs, which will be bearing the weight of the body above them. The arms, too—although not weight-bearing —will be "free" and therefore they will need support or strengthening at least. You must create a wire armature (page 53) on which to pack the clay. Because this armature—of lead or metal foil wire—must be flexible, it would collapse unless it were properly supported. So, instead of standing the wire skeleton on its own, you will hang it on a bent iron rod entering firmly at the point which will be the lumbar region of the figure. This is the part of the armature that is held firmly. The rest of the armature is left quite movable. This solid and stationary part of the armature (the gibbet) looks like an upside-down L. The horizontal and the upright are joined by an elbow. The upright pipe should be about nineteen inches long with the horizontal pipe measuring about nine inches and ending with a sideways T, from which the figure will be suspended. The middle part of the figure will be just below this T point. Allow for a two-inch-thick base on which your figure will stand. Make sure this base is level. Also make sure the board on which you have attached the iron rod with flanges and screws is thick and sturdy and will not warp. You can ensure against warping by painting or giving it a coat of some waterproofing material. Also shellac your iron rod (gibbet) to prevent it from rusting. Note that this rod is screwed down into one corner of the board and not in the middle. It must be so arranged that your figure will be suspended in the middle of the board.

Now create your skeleton with your wire. Twist it and pass it through the T. Twist the wire at the neck and the waist and spread it out at the rib cage and the hips. Make a loop up and down the thorax and come out for the arms, rather than across the shoulders. In this way, each arm will be independent of the other. After you have done this, adjust it and bind it carefully to the middle of the armature. Make certain of this, for it can be quite discouraging to have the armature move and wiggle, working itself loose inside. This is most disheartening to have happen when you have done a lot of work on your clay model.

Twist some additional wire around the leg part of the armature or the heavy clay masses will slip off.

If the figure will be weight-bearing on the right leg, then a line from the front of the inner ankle bone of this leg will be perpendicular to the pit of the neck; a line from the back of the seventh cervical must be perpendicular to the inner ankle bone. If the figure's stance is changed, the central line will change. And if the weight is equally distributed, the central line will fall equidistant between the feet.

Once you have the clay solidly packed to form the torso, work out to the arms and legs. Designate the line of the spine down the back and a corresponding one down the front of the torso from the pit of the neck to the symphysis. Don't forget to note the direction of the thorax as it counters the pelvic box and, of course, the area in between. Put a deep line across from one hip to the other (anterior iliac spines). This line across will be at right angles to the median line and will establish the swing of the pelvis. The leg bearing the weight will push up the hip above it and should be higher than the other relaxed hip.

In back, make a deep line indicating the S-swing of the vertebrae. Also indicate the shoulder blades. Take measurements. Measure from your level base to knees, from knees to symphysis; from symphysis to navel; from navel to arch of the rib cage, to pit of the neck, to chin, to the top of the head. Next, measure across the shoulders, hips, and all around. Step back and take a long critical look. Really look all around from the sides, from the back, from the front—once again. Look at the figure from the side, and note the diagonal directions of the thorax and the pelvis. Note how the profile all the way down curves back and forth and in and out in flowing rhythm. From the front, too, the lines are anything but straight. There will also be flat planes and deep areas, but the curves give the

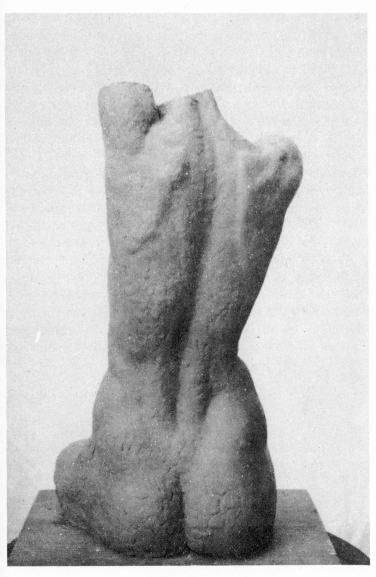

Illus. 115.

soft, graceful swing that is so important. Once you have this, then get the definite hard points of your bone structure. Ankles, knees, hipbones, shoulders, elbows. Note the big, flat plane areas. Keep building your figure up by putting clay upon clay until you arrive at the final size and shape you have planned. Remember that no matter what pose or shape your figure takes, there is always the same equal amount or bulk on each side of your central lines in back and in front. Remember also that muscles come around from the middle of the back, twist forward and around the ribs (latissimus) and from the waist to the back of the ribs (obliques). So it is difficult to say exactly where the front stops and the back begins. Look at your work from different eye levels. Also look at the corresponding part on the other side of the figure. Correlate. Be observant, alert. Work in different lights; change the source. Use a mirror for another view. These instructions and pointers will help you to bring your sculpture to a successful and satisfactory completion. The discipline that you will have acquired by this time will make your next sculpture less tedious, but the sense of elation and accomplishment will always be there with each and every figure you make.

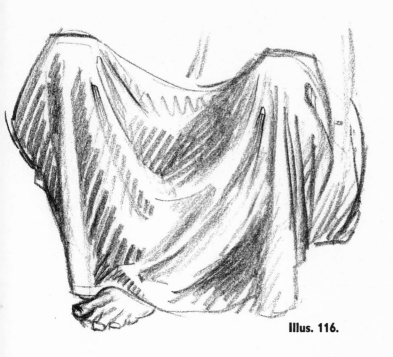

Illus. 116.

12. Draping the Figure

You may eventually want to do a draped or covered figure. The thing to remember is that there is as much anatomy in the cloth or drapery as there is in the figure beneath it. First, try draping different kinds of cloth by tacking them on the wall and copy the folds. The various weights and textures of materials will cause them to hang or fold differently.

When you drape the living figure, each time your model moves, the fall and folds of the cloth will change. Consequently, it is better to tack a piece of cloth on to a board and copy the folds and drapings (Illustration 117). Imitate. Begin by making a thick, long bat of clay and bend it sharply. Notice how this peaks up high where it has been bent. This high ridge, or upthrust, is what happens in every fold. Re-arrange the folds. Simplify them; make them look more sculptural. Later use a small manikin and drape it. Once you have posed it the way you like, tack the cloth on. If it is very thin material, dip it in water in which a few drops of glue have been added and then drape your dummy. The folds will dry and stay as you arranged them. You may want to eliminate the smaller or lesser folds.

The thing to remember is that the figure is modelled first and the drapery is added on. But this covering must have its own innate aesthetic value (Illustration 117). It must show the form beneath and not become a part of it. Don't smooth it down or in. Use drapery to enhance, to decorate, to lend charm and dignity. Poor drapery can cancel out all of your work on the figure.

Don't become discouraged. Once you've gotten the general idea of folds and drapery, you will be interpreting it in reference to the material (stone, marble, bronze, alabaster, etc.) for which you intend your sculpture. This is important. The treatment of drapery in marble will differ from its treatment in granite or limestone, etc. All this will come later after you have acquired the fundamentals in the technique of drapery.

Go to an art museum and study some of the magnificently draped and sculptured figures (Illustration 116). Note the rhythm of the folds, the fluting. See how they are used as design. Discover how drapery is treated in stone, how it is treated in wood. You will find the museum is a veritable treasure house of ideas if you will only come to it with an attitude of conscious attention and keen observation.

One last word of caution: Don't overdo drapery, don't become too literal, but—on the other hand—don't oversimplify and end up with nothing. As in the modelling of the figure,

Illus. 117. Pin a piece of cloth up on a board or wall. On another board, copy in clay the folds as they hang or fall. Folds will vary with the thickness and texture of the cloth. You can start by pinning up a bath towel, since it offers both thickness and texture.

there must always be thoughtful planning and preparatory sketches. Make the drape do the most for the form under it.

Illus. 118. Prepare for casting. Place shims, starting from the top of the head, behind the ears, down along the neck and shoulders.

13. Casting

Casting is not only a difficult job but also quite messy. Unless you have a studio or a special room you can use for this purpose, it is best to have a plaster caster do the casting for you. You can find the name of a professional caster from your school art department, art schools, plasterers, or monument dealers. If you do attempt it yourself, try a very small piece or a head at most. Prepare the area by covering the floor and everything else in the room with newspapers. Wear a smock or other protective clothing.

Powdered plaster has the peculiar property of whisking itself through the air and settling as a thick white dust everywhere, even in adjoining rooms.

If all of this has not discouraged you, then prepare the following items for the making of a mould:

> 25 pounds of casting plaster
> 2 mixing bowls, a large one and a small one
> 1 large spoon, bottle of liquid blueing, household oil, liquid soap
> 2 chisels, some brushes, piece of burlap
> 1 scraper, 1 hammer, some plaster tools.

Have all these items on a separate covered table beside your casting stand. Dip your spoon and bowls in cooking or olive oil. If you are going to cast a head or other three-dimensional

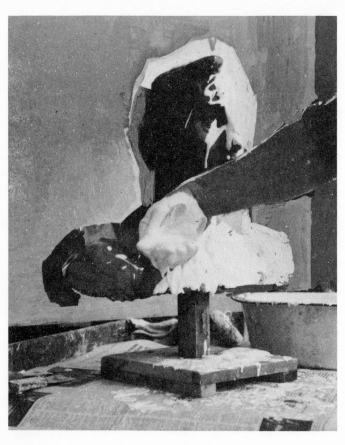

Illus. 119. Scoop up liquid plaster and fling it on to the clay model until the front is covered completely. A thickness of ¾ inch generally, but thicker at seams, is desirable.

piece, it cannot be done in one piece but must be cast in two sections. The back of the head is sectioned off. The sectioning is done by using shims, which are small metal strips about 1½ by 3 inches. The professional sculptor uses snippers to cut these metal shims to the size and shape he needs.

These small metal shims are inserted into the clay head all around, starting from the top of the head, down the sides, through the temples, behind the ears and vertically down the sides of the neck (Illustration 118). Cover the back of the head with tissue paper so it won't get splattered while you are plastering the front part of the mould.

Into the water of the large mixing bowl put two tablespoons of liquid laundry blueing which can be obtained in liquid form or made from powder. Now, into this blue water, very carefully sift some plaster, enough of it until it comes to the surface. Not more than that, otherwise your plaster will be too thick. Use your spoon to stir, but don't lift it out. Stir under until it looks like thick blue cream. Now dip the smaller bowl into the mixture and get some of the plaster out. From your smaller bowl, scoop some plaster in your hand and fling it gently but firmly on to the front half of your clay model (Illustration 119). The plaster may run off; catch it as it does and throw it back on. Continue until you have a thin coat all over the front. This colored film of plaster will guide you later on.

Blow gently with your mouth so that the plaster runs definitely into the nostrils and eyes and other deep places. Make sure every single part of the surface is covered (under the chin too). Put extra plaster all around the edge in front of the shims. Make a thick wall edging. This must be strengthened. It is very important to build up this thick seam. Scrape the plaster off the edges of the shims with your scraper. They must be clear so they can be pulled out later.

The plaster will now have begun to set. If you have any left over in your bowl, scrape it out and discard it. There will always be some wastage, but this is to be preferred over not having mixed enough plaster. Scrape your bowl clean. If some plaster still adheres, bend the rim of your bowl inward towards the middle and this will loosen it.

Illus. 120. The front has been completely covered with its first thin layer of plaster.

After your plaster has set enough and is beyond the smeary stage, you can brush it all over lightly with oil.

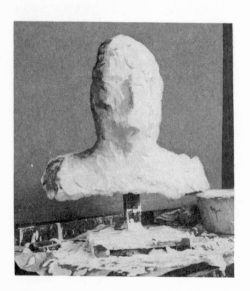

Illus. 121. Mix a second batch of plaster and cover. This should be a thicker mixture, the consistency of whipped cream.

Now mix a second batch of plaster, this time without the blueing and thicker in consistency than the first coat. Add this as an outer shell, which should be about an inch thick (Illustration 121). Dip some burlap strips in the plaster and bind them around the shell. (This is not really necessary on a small piece of sculpture.)

Once again clean and grease your bowl. Remove the tissue paper from the back of the clay head. If you view your model from in back you will note the one-inch edge of plaster all around the top of the head and vertically down the sides. In this plaster rim edge (from which you must remove the

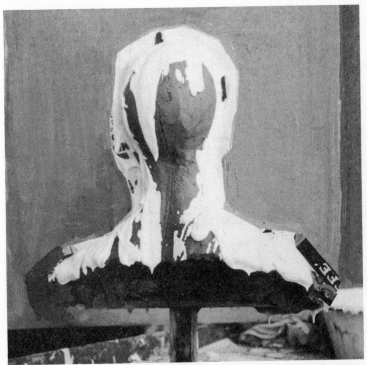

Illus. 122. View showing the plaster rim edge as the process is repeated on the back of the head.

shims with pincers), cut some small notches with a little knife or spatula. These notches are called keys. Make them V-shaped. They will serve to fit the two sections of the mould together later when you have the second section of the mould cast.

Grease the $1\frac{1}{2}$-inch edge carefully. Now begin again as you did for the front (Illustration 122). Put blueing in the water and mix plaster and complete all of the steps as you did before.

Allow thirty minutes to about an hour for the plaster to set. Next, pry the two sections apart. Ease a thin chisel into the seam (but not near a key). Use gentle pressure back and forth. When the mould starts to open put a knife blade on each side and gently and gradually pull the back section away from the front. By this time you should be able to lift it away without difficulty. Do not worry about having "destroyed" your clay figure. You have preserved it in plaster.

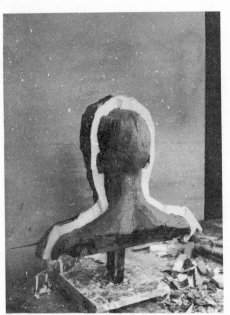

Illus. 123. When the plaster has set for up to one hour, pry the two sections apart at the seam where the shims were inserted. Remove the inside clay model from the plaster moulds.

When you have separated the two sections, begin to dig out the clay from inside your mould (Illustration 124). Use a blunt tool. Try to keep the clay as clean and free from plaster bits as possible because you will be re-using the clay for your next piece of sculpture. Also have a receptacle or box ready in which to store it.

Before you have gotten all the clay out you will reach the armature, which you must remove from the mould very carefully, so as to not cause any damage to the plaster. Remove any clay that remains gently. If you have used plastilene (oil-based clay), water will not dissolve it from the deep or tiny crevices. Nevertheless, you must remove every trace of clay from your mould without damaging or scratching it.

After the two sections have been cleaned, they must be soft-soaped or shampooed. With a soft brush, work the soap (boil one part soap and three parts water) over every single part of your mould. You must do this for about ten minutes. The entire surface must be covered. (Don't forget the ears.) Let the mould soak for about fifteen minutes; then remove the soap. With your brush, pick up the soap. Each time you do, squeeze it from your brush with your fingers. Repeat this over and over until you have picked up all the soap. Now you can very lightly brush on a few drops of oil but only on the high points.

When you have the two sections of the mould clean, soaped, and oiled you can use either of two methods for making a cast. You can pour each section separately or you can bind both together as one shell and pour the plaster into the entire unit.

If you are going to do each section separately, you mix enough plaster to line the moulds about one inch thick. Don't stir the plaster too long or it will set too fast. If you want to fill both sections immediately, you will have to work rapidly without interruptions. Pour in only a little at first, then tilt and twirl the mould so the plaster gets in and around everywhere (Illustration 124). Blow the plaster into every crevice. Keep the seam clean, but cover the mould thoroughly.

Illus. 124. After cleaning the mould sections thoroughly (and removing all traces of soap), pour new plaster into the moulds for your cast.

After both sections are filled with an inch of plaster, clap the two sections together firmly, fitting the two sections into the notched keys. Now dip burlap (2×3-inch pieces) into thick plaster and place these sopped patches along the seam for

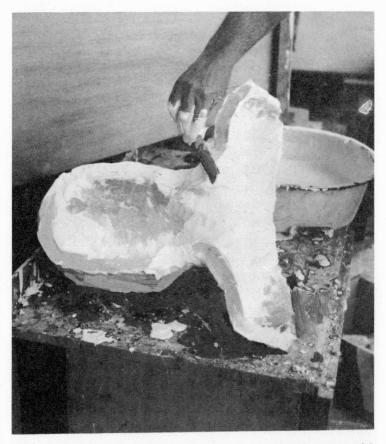

Illus. 125. Before the plaster is completely set, clean the edges with a blunt tool so the two halves will fit together.

reinforcement—at the top of the head, several others on each side; others on the neck. You can also tie the two sections together with cord, but the burlap patches should be enough to hold them firmly together.

There is another method of plaster casting. After you have

cleaned and soaped the mould, fit the two sections together and put strips of burlap dipped in plaster along the seam. This is an open-bottom hollow shell. Stand it upside down on the table. Put a support under it so it won't tip over or move. (You can wind a thick old towel and encircle your upturned mould to keep it steady.) Mix the plaster, dip some out with the smaller bowl and pour it into the shell, tilting and turning around and around gently but firmly so the plaster covers the entire inside surface. Make sure there is a goodly layer over all. Don't fill the head. You can drip out some of the loose, running plaster as you go along.

Repeat pouring, more slowly, allowing the consecutive layers of plaster to set. Tip out the excess. When you think you have a one-inch-thick cast you can stop pouring and twirling. Wait about an hour or so. In the meantime you can be clearing away the trash and splattered newspapers to get ready for the chipping.

Once again spread clean newspapers around and on the stand and on the floor. Get set to chip away the outside shell. With a mallet and a dull chisel tap away the burlap strips you have placed around the seam. Don't chip too deep and don't force your tools. Begin at the seam and slowly remove the outer shell. Hold the chisel in place at right angles resting your hand against it and tap it with the mallet. Pull your chisel back as soon as it cracks the plaster. The white outer shell will gradually chip and crack and come off in pieces (Illustration 126). Sometimes large pieces will come off with one stroke. Sometimes the blue layer may be still left attached to the cast. Remove this gently with a light tap on your chisel. If some small blue patches remain in the ears or nostrils, you can use a plaster tool to get them out. Always proceed with caution. Always be ready to pull your chisel away. The back of the head is usually easy to chip and uncover, coming off in one or two big pieces.

Illus. 126. Gently chip away the mould from the cast. Use a dull chisel cautiously. Tap the chisel gently with a mallet. Repeat until the entire cast is released.

Take extra care around the ears. You can easily snap them off and ruin your work. Use a smaller chisel, gently.

Don't be discouraged if you dig or nick your cast. This happens sometimes to the most experienced casters. Minor repairs or patching should be done as soon as possible while the cast is still fresh and moist.

To patch, mix a small amount of casting plaster in a halved

hollow rubber ball. This makes a very useful and very easily cleaned receptacle. Sift the plaster into the water; don't stir. Allow it to stand. Run a knife through the mixture. If the cut does not disappear but remains visible, the plaster is ready to be used for filling in or patching. Before you apply the plaster go over the damaged spot, applying water with a wet brush. Make sure your patching plaster is properly prepared as described above; otherwise, your patched areas will dry out darker and harder than the rest of the cast.

There are, of course, other kinds and methods of casting. For example, there is casting by means of a glue mould or a piece mould. These are best left to expert casters. They are complex, smelly, and messy and seldom attempted even by professional sculptors.

Of course, bronze casting must be done at a foundry. If your piece of sculpture is going to be cast in bronze, then you will deliver the plaster cast (positive replica) to the foundry, where experts in molten metal will pour and cast it for you. The bronze cast is made hollow, about $\frac{1}{4}$ inch thick. It is a difficult, intricate and expensive process. If you arrange to visit a foundry, you will find it a very interesting place, and you will also realize just how complicated the bronze casting process is.

14. Textures

Texture refers to the degree of smoothness or roughness of the surface. You can treat your clay so it will have a smooth texture by eliminating all of the irregularities on its surface. Or you may prefer to have a rough or bumpy surface, in which case you can show how you have applied each pellet; you may want a very symmetrically indented or striated surface; or you may want to treat the hair, for example, in a classic manner with each curl or strand exactly alike.

The next time you visit an art exhibit, take note of the different textures used by sculptors. You will find that the sculptor Jean Arp, for example, uses smooth, almost glasslike surfaces for his marble pieces; Brancusi uses smooth surfaces for his metal sculpture; Jacques Lipschitz and Sir Jacob Epstein each use rough, almost jagged surface textures for their bronzes, while other sculptors like José de Creeft use mixed surface textures, with part of the piece smooth and another part done in a rough texture.

At museums and galleries observe the textures used by Stone Age sculptors, the Etruscan, the Egyptian, the Greek and Roman, the Byzantine, the Romanesque, the Gothic, the Renaissance, the eighteenth and nineteenth century sculptors; study the textures used by Auguste Rodin, Jean Baptiste Carpeaux, Antonio Canova, Henry Moore, Marino Marini, Viani, Mastroianni, Castelli and Lynn Chadwick; such observation will add to your knowledge of sculpture in general and of texture in particular.

The thing to remember is that there are innumerable degrees of smoothness or roughness and combinations of textures that can be used. Whatever texture you use must add clarity and aesthetic value to the expression of your ideas in sculpture.

15. Finishes

If you are planning to display your plaster cast, there are a number of ways in which you can give it a very attractive finish. If you want an ivory finish you can paint it with two coats of shellac. Mix 2 parts of white shellac (4-pound cut) with 1½ parts of alcohol. Use a clean brush; don't overload it. Start from the top of the head and work down evenly. Let it dry for an hour before you apply the second coat. You can add a bit of dry powdered color to the second coat of shellac; some sepia or yellow ochre will do. This will make your cast darker. You can get a soft, glowing effect by going over your cast with melted beeswax thinned out with turpentine.

If you want to give your cast a bronze finish, apply two coats of alcohol wood stain; one in dark oak color and the other in redwood. On the second coat of wet wood stain, brush some bronze powder very lightly and mostly on high points. After this is thoroughly dry, you can add a coat of wax and polish it with a soft cloth.

Bronzing is not a method for which specific directions can be given. You must experiment, and in the process you may come off with a magnificently unexpected result.

Try a green-tinted bronze finish. First, give the cast a coat of shellac. Next, mix some dry apple-green color with shellac and brush it on. You can apply additional colored powder with a soft piece of cloth. Touch your cast gently with it wherever you want it to adhere. Shake it on or puff it on. If you have some bare spots cover them with the beeswax and turpentine mixture and then puff on the green powder. Remove any excess with a clean soft brush. You can always tone down the color or add to it, but don't make it uniformly green. Mix some blue to it; apply it unevenly. The more variations there are, the more closely it will look like green bronze.

To get a stone-finished quality, give your cast a coat of shellac followed by a coat of grey paint. Now, in a fixative blower, place liquid show card colors, blue, white, pink, yellow, one at a time. With plenty of blowing power, blow droplets of each color on to your cast. (Don't spray the objects around you. Do it carefully.) There are other ways of duplicating a stone finish, but this is the only one found to be quick and satisfactory.

You can also use light, plastic spray colors. You will need a number of spray cans because each contains a single color. Spray each color on consecutively. Gently, cautiously, sparingly.

For a granite-like finish, first shellac your cast, then follow with a thin coat of grey house paint. Now dip a large stiff brush into a darker grey paint but don't brush it on. Stand about a foot or two away from your cast and hold the brush up in your right hand. Now, in your left hand hold a wood slat the size of a foot rule. Draw this slat across the loaded paint brush bristles so that larger paint droplets fall on your cast. Clean the brush and dip it into other colors, ranging from blues to ochres. Your choice of colors will vary with the type of granite you are trying to simulate.

You can also try a marble finish. This requires much work and judgment. Your cast must be thoroughly dry. Go over the entire surface with a rasp, accenting forms and decorations. With plaster tools you can model directly on the cast. This requires both craftsmanship and modelling ability. With fine emery paper go over and smooth the surface until it becomes as close to a polished marble texture as possible. For a high sheen sprinkle with powdered talc, and polish the cast vigorously with a soft cloth.

There are many and various finishes which you can experiment with, if you will not be discouraged and if you are adventurous to take a chance on the outcome. Most finishes can be renewed without much damage to the cast. You can lighten, darken, smooth or roughen them.

16. Some Larger Sculptures

All by Louis di Valentin

Illus. 127. "Mother and Child."

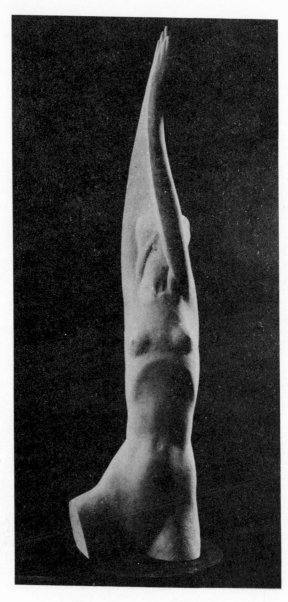

Illus. 128. "Jeune Fille."

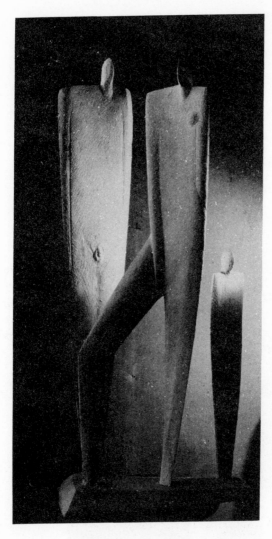

Illus. 129. "Family."

Illus. 130.
"Joseph"
in Chapel- Holyoke,
Holyoke,
Massachusetts.

Illus. 131.
"Mary and Jesus"
in Chapel-Holyoke,
Holyoke,
Massachusetts.

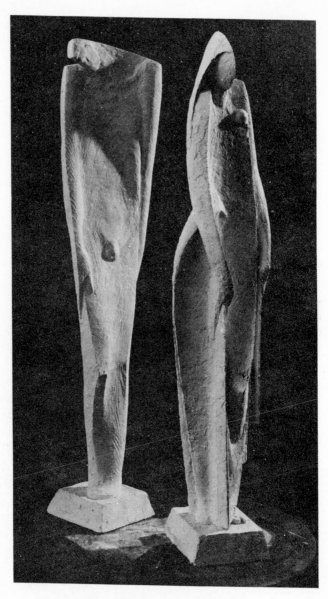

Illus. 132. "Male and Female."

17. Bas-Relief

Bas-relief is sometimes defined as sculptured drawing, or raised drawing. It has the dimensions of length and breadth, but its third dimension, depth, varies. It varies from bas- (or low) relief to haut- (or high) relief; high relief may project from the background to almost fully round proportions.

A good bas-relief requires the knowledge and execution of good drawing. The sculptor must be adept in draftmanship, in the use of charcoal and pencil, to draw at least the outline of his subject, whether it be a profile of a head or of the entire body. In this chapter, we will show you how to do a bas-relief portrait. However, you can apply the same basic procedures to any bas-relief.

To begin your portrait, outline on paper, with pencil or charcoal, the profile of the sitter's head. Note the various proportions of the facial features and relate them to one another. Relate the distance from the brow to the top of the ear, remembering that they are horizontally in 'ine with each other. Line up the tip of the nose with the bottom of the ear, and place the back of the skull on the same horizontal line. Refer to previous chapters on facial anatomy. You will use your drawing as a guide for your work in clay.

On an easel, place an appropriate-sized shellacked wooden

Illus. 133. Set up your shellacked board on an easel and mark off the area for the bas-relief.

board upon which to pack and level the clay. With charcoal, mark out the area of the board which will contain the clay. On both the left and right sides of the marked-off area, nail a strip of wood to the board to set the thickness or depth of the clay background, which will be about ½ inch. Pack on your clay between the wooden strips to the level determined by them. Add the clay on the board little by little and bit by bit until the board is covered with an even distribution of clay.

Now take a straight-edge and, holding both ends, press down to draw it across the clay, diagonally from top to bottom, horizontally, and from left to right. Scrape down firmly. Draw the straight-edge over the surface of the clay until you obtain an even and level plane. Fill in any hollow places or spots with more clay where needed, and smooth out again.

With a wooden sculpture tool, copy the outlines of your drawn profile in the smooth-surfaced clay. Place the portrait outline in the clay, so that you leave more space in front of the face than in back. This is best for compositional purposes, so the profile will not look as if it were walking out of the designated area. Reliefs using figures must also be composed so they are well framed (Illustrations 147 to 149).

Cut away the background around the profile with a wire sculpture tool. This cutting away of the background must be performed very lightly and cautiously. It is done to give rise to your outlined profile. Eventually the entire background will be cut away to an even depth, which depends on how deeply you want to cut away at the nose outline, the front of the neck and the back of the head.

The next step is to add clay to build up the form. Use bits of clay that are well-worked and soft. Add to the high points on the skull first: the cheekbone, the outermost part of the forehead, the temple, the jaw. Use the thumb to establish these structural high points. Press the softened bits of clay on firmly, but do not press hard enough to dislodge the underlayer of clay. Use no tools, just the thumb.

Illus. 134. Nail wooden strips at the left and right boundaries and pack bits of clay in between the strips, building up a depth of $\frac{1}{2}$ inch.

Illus. 135. Firmly level the clay by drawing a straight-edge across it in various directions.

Illus. 136. Incise the outlines of your drawing into the smooth, clay surface with a wooden tool.

Illus. 137. Lightly scrape away a layer of clay around the outline of your subject with a wire tool. The profile is now in relief against the background, which will eventually be scraped to an even thickness all over.

Add clay to the middle planes formed by the medium structural points, such as the upper maxillary, the nostril, etc. Fill in all the middle planes, such as between the cheekbone and the jawbone. Add protruding points as the ear and shoulder. Note that, above the eye, the forehead is close to you, but that it recedes above the nose and becomes a lower plane. The closest point to you will be the highest. For example, the hair over the ear will be close to you, but as it goes towards the back of the skull, it recedes into a lower plane, so there will be less clay added. The shoulder, in profile, is the highest point because it is closest to you.

After placing the clay masses, define the planes more exactly, separating the areas closest to you from those furthermost from you. Use a flat wooden tool to do this.

The next to the last step is to model and blend the clay. Keep the planes distinct, but work one into the other smoothly. Refine and designate the planes and variations, but always keep the anatomical structure. Scrape away the background so it is level.

Last to be dealt with are the details, the many small planes and curves in the eye, the nose, the mouth, the ear. Every feature must be in proper relationship to the others. Observe that the shoulder is closest to you, then the hair, the ear, the jaw, the neck. The outer edge of the eye is closer than the inner edge, and vertically the inner edge of the eye lines up with the outermost part of the mouth. The tip of the nose and the mid-mouth are the farthest away in profile.

The most usual errors made by beginners are: the head is too close to the edge of the background; the head is curved concave where it should be convex; the inner corner of the eye is too deep; the nostril is set too deeply; the cheekbone is not noted sufficiently; the ear is set too low or too high; the under-lip and the chin are not separated; the anatomy of the neck has not been studied; the hair is not treated as a mass; the shoulder is not properly defined.

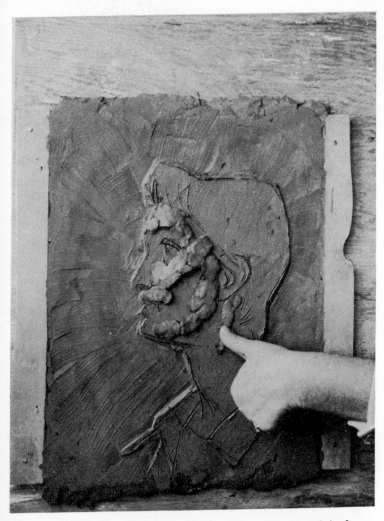

Illus. 138. Add small masses of soft clay to the high points of the face—such as the cheekbone, the jaw and the temple. Do not press so hard that you disturb the underlayer of clay.

Illus. 139. Form the medium structural points such as the nostril and the upper maxillary, then fill in all the areas between the high and medium points. Add the points closest to you—the shoulder, the hair, the ear.

Illus. 140. Using a flat, wooden tool, define the various planes of the face. Apply the anatomical knowledge you have gained in preceding chapters. Note, for instance, that the outer edge of the eye is closer to you than the inner edge.

Illus. 141. Blend the clay so that the planes are distinct but flow smoothly into one another. Treat the hair as a mass but begin adding details, such as the eye in its socket, the eyebrows, etc.

Illus. 142. Define and blend the many small planes of the ear, eye, nose and mouth. Soften the areas where medium, high and low planes intersect. Level the background, and your bas-relief is complete.

To avoid such errors, not only is good drawing helpful but so is a knowledge of anatomy. You should study your model as well as the pages in this book on the structure of the skull and head to learn the areas and divisions of the face—where the eyes are placed in relation to the nose; the nose to the mouth; and the mouth to the chin. You will be able to determine where the ears are set and how the lower jaw merges with the neck. In front, the neck is attached by two muscles to the breastbone. On the side, the neck comes down into the shoulder and it flows into the back from the base of the skull. The shape and form of each feature must be studied until learned and deeply appreciated.

In order to do a good bas-relief you must have the sort of training which is required for sculpture in the round, even if bas-relief does not present as many problems. The knowledge of handling clay as material is essential. You may also put to use your knowledge of casting plaster to make a permanent model of your clay relief.

INCISED BAS-RELIEF

Bas-relief may be produced by incising or carving away the clay surface rather than by adding to it. You begin in the same way with a drawing made on paper to be used as a guide while working in clay. Prepare a board as before with wooden side strips to contain the clay area. Level a smooth, clay surface about ¾-inch thick by drawing a straight-edge over the packed clay. With a wooden tool, outline the subject in the soft clay, drawing as you would with charcoal or pencil. Next, use a wire tool to cut down into the clay below the surface. The deepest cut is the outline; the shallowest cuts are those for the closest planes. In the case of the portrait shown in Illustrations 143 to 146, the nose, left cheekbone and forehead are the

Illus. 143. On smoothly-packed clay $\frac{3}{4}$ of an inch thick, draw your subject as before. This time, however, you will make an incised bas-relief; instead of adding to the surface, you will be cutting into it.

Illus. 144. Use a wire tool for cutting. Carve deeply around the outline to establish the most receding points—the top of the head, the right side of the subject's face, the hair on the left side, etc. Retain the high points—nose, left cheekbone, and forehead—on the original clay surface and make shallow cuts for planes in between.

Illus. 145. Model the structural planes with a wire tool. All modelling and cutting is done below the original clay surface.

Illus. 146. Refine and blend the modelled planes with a wooden tool. Attend to details last. Indicate hair with incised strokes.

Illus. 147. An incised bas-relief, 28 feet tall, by Louis di Valentin for the facade of the women's dormitory at Indiana University in Bloomington.

points closest to the observer; therefore they are retained at the original clay surface, untouched.

After you have made all your necessary cuts, model and blend the planes with a wire tool. Areas such as the neck, shoulders, inner corner of the eyes, under the eyes, and over the eyelids should get particular attention. All modelling and cutting is done below the original ¾-inch deep clay surface. Hair is suggested with indented strokes.

With a wooden tool, refine and designate the planes and areas. Lastly attend to details. Soften and blend the planes lightly.

Illus. 148. Opposite Page: the left, middle and right sections of a classic style bas-relief executed by Louis di Valentin for the home of Mrs. Theodore Eisendrath, Washington, D.C.

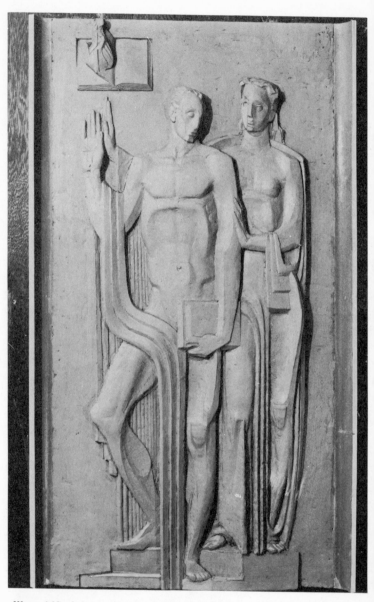

Illus. 149. A bas-relief by Louis di Valentin for Indiana University.

18. Caricature

Caricature is defined as a representation of a person or thing, drawn, painted or sculpted in a fanciful fashion with exaggeration or emphasis of a particular trait. Sometimes the intent is to ridicule or satirize the subject; other times the intent is to give a whimsical view of the subject. The subject shown here in step-by-step photographs is President Richard M. Nixon. The same preparations are made as for any other piece of sculpture.

On a worktable, place a board with an armature consisting of an upright wooden rectangle and a small block nailed to the upright. This block is used to hold the clay fast and prevent it from slipping off while you build up the form. Soften the clay somewhat by rolling it into sausage-like bats and pile the clay on the table near the board.

Press the clay on to the armature in the general shape intended (Illustration 150). The most projecting features have the most clay (the tip of the nose, the chin, etc.). The masses formed by the less prominent features—the brow and the cheeks, the mouth, the hair and the neck—come closer to the armature and farther away from you. Don't forget that you are exaggerating the subject's features.

Illus. 150. Mass the clay around your armature in the general form you intend the caricature to have. Remember you are exaggerating the most prominent features. Follow photographs of your subject (if not a live model) from various views as a guide.

182

Subtract clay where it is not needed, such as in the areas of the eye sockets, with a round, wire tool (Illustration 151). Model the masses into the various planes of the face with a wooden sculpture tool. Different size wire and wooden tools are used according to the purpose they serve. The wooden tool helps to separate the underlip from the upper chin (Illustration 153). Modelling requires an in-and-out movement and a rounding and blending technique. The nostril is set into the face; so are the corners of the mouth and the inner corners of the eyes.

The planes of the face should be defined; the eye is on a different plane than the brow, the hair, the ears, etc. In profile, the relationships of brow, eye and ear; of hair, brow, nose; and of mouth, chin, under-chin and neck become quite obvious (Illustration 154).

Details, such as wrinkles on the brow, are always left for the last. Sometimes, they are handled best by suggestion. For instance, the hair has been treated as a wavy mass rather than by accenting the individual hairs (Illustration 152).

You may cast your caricatures in the same way as other sculptures. In the case of a high relief, however, such as the caricature of Albert Einstein (Illustration 156), the casting method is altered somewhat.

You model your caricature on a vertical board to which a block of wood has been nailed and upon which you mass your clay in the shape you want. Proceed to refine your sculpture. When ready for casting the clay model into plaster, you remove the board from its easel and put the board down flat on a surface which has been cautiously covered and protected by newspapers. Plaster in a creamy, liquid consistency is poured evenly over the clay. (See chapter on casting.)

When an inch-thick plaster covering has been poured, allow the plaster to dry, forming a mould. Remove it by inserting a spatula all around the edges and lifting the plaster form from the board. You then remove the clay from the back of the

Illus. 151 Use a wire tool to scoop out areas of unnecessary clay, such as where the eye sockets will be. Establish the placement of features just as you would in doing a portrait head, with the ears lined up between the tip of the nose and the brow, etc.

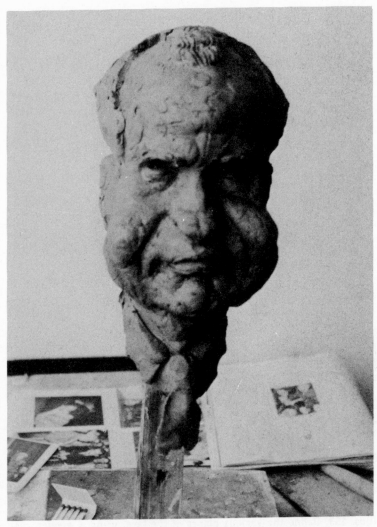

Illus. 152. The accented characteristics of the subject, President Richard M. Nixon, are already apparent in the heavy jowls, the sloped nose and the receding hairline.

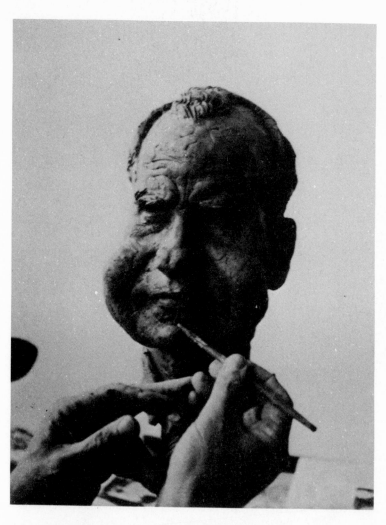

Illus. 153. Define the various planes of the face, using a wooden tool to model and blend the clay. Here the tool is being used to separate the underlip from the upper chin.

Illus. 154. In profile, the relationship of each part of the face to the other parts becomes obvious. Note, for instance, that the inner corner of the eye is on a vertical line with the outer corner of the mouth.

Illus. 155. The caricature of President Franklin D. Roosevelt by Louis di Valentin accents the sharp, long nose, the indented mouth and jutting chin, the fleshy underchin and heavy neck. The amiable smile forces jovial wrinkles at the outer edges of the eyes, and from under the chin to the cheek.

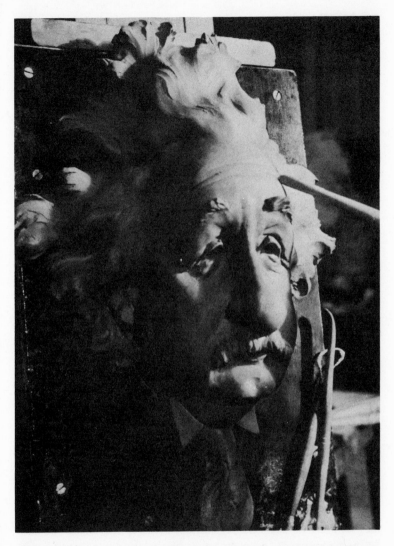

Illus. 156. This caricature of Albert Einstein, by Louis di Valentin, is an exaggeration of the characteristics of his wildly abundant hair, his droopy eyes and mouth, and his rather prominent nose. The mustache shadows and covers a small mouth.

mould. This plaster mould is a negative of the clay model. When it has been thoroughly cleaned of the clay, you brush it with liquid soap.

The negative plaster mould is now coated inside (to a 2-inch thickness) with a creamy, liquid plaster. When the cast in the mould has dried, chip away the outer mould with a mallet and small chisel.

Making caricatures is one of the most rewarding uses to which you can put your knowledge of sculpture, but as in other cases you must be familiar with facial anatomy. With practice, you will succeed.

INDEX